296.431
B23   Barish, Louis.
a   High Holiday liturgy.

Temple Israel
Library
Minneapolis, Minn.

––––––––

Please sign your full name on the above card.

Return books promptly to the Library or Temple Office.

Fines will be charged for overdue books or for damage or loss of same.

HIGH HOLIDAY LITURGY

High Holiday
LITURGY

by

RABBI LOUIS BARISH

JONATHAN DAVID

Publishers   New York

HIGH HOLIDAY LITURGY
Copyright 1959
by LOUIS BARISH

Library of Congress Catalog Card No. 59-10540

PRINTED IN THE UNITED STATES OF AMERICA

THIS BOOK IS

DEDICATED TO

MY BELOVED WIFE

REBECCA

WHO SPURRED MY EFFORTS

AND CHEERED MY PROGRESS

CONTENTS

PREFACE

The *Machzor* is an abundant treasure. Its priceless psychological insights, profound ideas, spiritual and moral ideals, and realistic approach can add meaning and purpose, and suggest direction, to a life worth living. The Jew, searching for an answer to the question, "Does life have meaning?" would do well to turn to the *Machzor* for guidance.

The *Machzor* can, and should, be a very meaningful Jewish experience. Yet, the best translations cannot make the mind comprehend, nor the spirit quicken to, its vital force which *could* invest each life with true worth and significance. There is a need for commentaries to unlock its innumerable insights which can enhance life but often lie hidden in a shrine of sublime poetry, and obscure phraseology and references, which is the High Holiday Prayerbook.

Today, the Jew is separated from his heritage, the wisdom of the *Machzor,* by a whole universe of discourse. This heritage needs to be interpreted in terms of the specific needs and thought patterns of contemporary life. My desire is to encourage appreciation for the *Machzor* by providing the student and worshipper with a method for analysis and interpretation of our wonderfully precious prayers. More specifically, my object is to provide helpful information and enlarged understanding in the following areas: order of the prayers, names of the prayers, history of the prayers, psychological values and theological principles of the prayers, laws and procedures governing rendition of the prayers and the biographies of the great poets who were inspired to create the prayers.

This commentary is intended for the layman. It is hoped that individuals and groups, students and worshippers, will find it useful. The ideas and subject matter can be of interest to the general reader without reference to the *Machzor* text. To facilitate its use by study circles, adult classes and laymen's institutes, I have prepared a study guide which is available from the publisher on request. This guide recommends, and outlines, four distinct approaches:

1. Systematic service by service study
2. Theology of the *Machzor*
3. Psychology of the *Machzor*
4. History of the *Machzor*

After each prayer that is being discussed the reader will find the letters A, B and S followed by a page number. These refer to pages in the following High Holiday Prayer Books:

A—Adler's "Service of the Synagogue—New Year and Day of Atonement" (One or two volume edition).
B—Birnbaum's "High Holy Day Prayer Book."
S—Silverman's "High Holiday Prayer Book."

I wish to express my appreciation and indebtedness to Dr. Solomon B. Freehof, visiting Professor of Homiletics and Liturgy at Hebrew Union College, to Dr. Robert Gordis, Professor of Bible at the Jewish Theological Seminary of America, and to Dr. Sidney Hoenig, Director of the Adult Education Department of Yeshiva University, who read the proofs and from whom I drew much wisdom and inspiration.

LOUIS BARISH

July 1, 1959
Fort Hamilton
New York

1

What Is the Machzor?

The *Machzor* is a book of faith. In it is expressed the conviction that what ought to be, *can* be:

A world scarred by sin *can* be healed by virtue.
Man divided within himself *can* be whole.
Men estranged from each other *can* discover their
    essential oneness.
Nations torn by conflict *can* achieve unity.

The *Machzor* is also a book of prayerful prophesy. In it is expressed the expectation that what can be, *will* be:

"Iniquity shall close its mouth and all wickedness
    vanish like smoke."
"On this day Thou dost lovingly plead with us: Cast
    away all your transgressions and make you
    a new heart and a new spirit . . . that ye
    may live."
"O make an end of blood, shed by man, and wash the
    stain away. . . . May all Thy children unite
    in one humanity to do Thy will."
"And the world will be perfected under Thine
    Almighty Kingdom."

WHAT MACHZOR MEANS

Machzor means cycle. Originally the *Machzor* contained all the services of the annual cycle. Today the *Machzor* is the Prayer Book comprising only services for the High Holidays or for the three major festivals. We have a *Machzor* for the *Yomim Noraim* (the Days of Awe: Rosh Hashanah and Yom Kippur). We have another *Machzor* for the *Sholosh Regolim* (the three Pilgrimage Festivals: *Pesach, Shevuos, Sukkos*).

The word *Machzor* comes from a Hebrew root *chazor* which means to return or to repeat. The Prayer Book is called *Machzor* (cycle) because the Holy Days *return* to us every year and because we *repeat* the services associated with them when they *recur*.

THE HISTORY OF THE MACHZOR

In ancient times the Bible was known as the Written Law. Everything else, namely, the rabbinic discussions and amplifications of the Law, the post-biblical literature, the services of the synagogue, etc., were considered part of the Oral Tradition. It was forbidden to write down any part of the Oral Tradition to insure the position of authority of the Written Law. Thus, there were no prayer books. The leader of the service recited the prayers from memory. By approximately 500 C.E., it was universally apparent that the Oral Tradition was too unwieldy for oral transmission from generation to generation. Consequently, the ban on writing it down was removed in order to preserve this great heritage, and prayer books came into being.

The early prayer books were simply collections of special groups of prayers and of laws governing their proper use. The "Hundred Benedictions," written by Gaon Natronai, is an example of this type of early prayer book. Another Gaon, Amram, wrote a "Compendium of Prayers and Blessings for the Entire Year." "Prayers and Songs of Prayers," compiled by Gaon Saadiah, was more complete. It included notes, textual references, interpretations of the prayers, and the rules governing their use.

As time passed, the newer prayer books developed into compendia of the religious life of the Jew, describing and explaining the annual cycle of Jewish religious requirements, and came to be called *Machzor* (cycle). The best known and most complete of the *Machzorim* was written in the 12th century by Simcha ben Samuel, a disciple of the School of Rashi. "Machzor Vitry," so-called because Simcha ben Samuel lived and wrote in the city of Vitry, contains prayers and their explanations, rules governing the order of the service, scriptural readings, features of the calendar, and prescriptions regulating the manufacture of ritual objects. It begins with the laws, customs, and prayers for the weekday services; treats the Sabbath Services similarly; and covers fully the liturgy for the Holy Days. This Machzor Vitry was used by later scholars in the construction of our present-day *Siddurim* (Daily Prayer Books) and *Machzorim* (Festival Prayer Books).

THE ORDER OF THE HIGH HOLIDAY SERVICES

Rosh Hashanah

Maariv	—	Evening Service
Shachris	—	Morning Service
Musaf	—	Additional Service
Mincha	—	Afternoon Service

Yom Kippur

Maariv	—	Evening Service (*Kol Nidre*)
Shachris	—	Morning Service (*Yizkor*)
Musaf	—	Additional Service
Mincha	—	Afternoon Service
Neila	—	Concluding Service

3

THE DATES OF THE PRAYERS

The *Machzor* contains the above services in the order indicated. Some of the prayers in these services date back to the earliest days of Jewish history. Others came into being during the period of the first Temple, 925-586 B.C.E. Most of them were either composed or edited in their present form during the early days of the second Temple, 516 B.C.E.-70 C.E. In addition to these older, familiar types of prayers which are predominant in the *Siddur,* the *Machzor* has two special types of prayers which appear only occasionally in the daily prayer book but very frequently in the services of the High Holy Days, to wit, *piyutim* and *selichos.*

PIYUTIM—POEMS

The word for poems is *piyutim.* The authors of these synagogal poems were known as *paitanim.* Both words come from the Greek, *poietrie* and *poietes.* The first *piyutim,* written during the 8th century and perhaps even in the 7th century, are anonymous. The oldest known *paitan* was Joe ben Jose who lived not later than 850 C.E. The next known *paitan* was Yannai, the teacher of the most prolific poet, Eliezer ben Kalir. Saadiah Gaon in the 10th century was the most famous philosophical poet. From that time on, poets of the synagogue became very numerous. Even Maimonides, the great Jewish philosopher, was known to have written some *piyutim.* The historian Zunz identifies over 900 of them. After the 14th century this type of poetry declined, and in the 18th century disappeared completely.

Many of the rabbis were opposed to the insertion of the *piyutim* into the Service. They regarded them as interruptions in the sacred liturgy, and disliked the unaesthetic anthropomorphism which crops up frequently in these poems. They were particularly unsympathetic toward *piyutim* heavily ornamented with angelology and philosophical overstatement. The rabbis, preferring the simple, concise style of the biblical and talmudic

4

prayers, yielded reluctantly to the popular demand for the *piyutim* among the people. Thus, despite rabbinic opposition, many mystical and highly philosophical *piyutim* found their way into the liturgy of the synagogue.

SELICHOS

Many of the prayers in the *Machzor* are called *selichos*. The word *selichos* means penitential prayers, prayers in which we ask God's forgiveness. These prayers are recited daily during the month of Elul (30 days) and during the Ten Days of Repentance, from the first of Tishri (Rosh Hashanah) through the 10th of Tishri (Yom Kippur). These 40 days correspond to the 40 days spent by Moses and the people in repentance over the broken tablets of the law. At midnight after the Sabbath preceding Rosh Hashanah, a special service called *selichos* is held, unless the interval between that Sabbath and Rosh Hashanah is less than 4 days. In the latter event, the midnight *selichos* service is held one week earlier. The special prayer book for this service is also called *selichos*. Each morning of the remaining days before Rosh Hashanah, we recite these special penitential prayers called *selichos*.

It was said that every morning during the week before Rosh Hashanah the rabbi of Nemirov, at *selichos* time, disappeared . . . melted into thin air. He was not to be found anywhere, either in the synagogue or in the House of Study, and most certainly not at his home. His door stood open and people came and went as they pleased, but the rabbi was not to be seen. The rumor quickly spread that the rabbi ascended to heaven to plead before the Almighty for his people.

Once, a shrewd Litvak came to town. When he heard the story of the rabbi's disappearance, he shrugged his shoulders, laughed a little, and secretly resolved to discover the truth and to expose the rabbi of Nemirov.

One night before Rosh Hashanah, the Lithuanian stole into the rabbi's room and lay down under the rabbi's bed intending to stay there all night if necessary to find out what the rabbi did and where he went to *selichos*. Day had not yet broken when he was suddenly awakened by the voice of the rabbi chanting his morning prayers. After his prayers, the rabbi dressed himself in rude peasant dress, put a hatchet under his peasant belt, and left the house. The Lithuanian followed him through the side streets and the shadows of the houses until he emerged from town. Behind the town stood a forest which the rabbi entered. It was still dark and hard to see but this the Lithuanian did see . . . he saw the rabbi take out his hatchet, chop down a tree, split it into kindling wood, make a bundle of it, and fling it over his shoulder. The rabbi started back to town, followed by the Lithuanian. The rabbi stopped in a back street of the poor gentile section before a humble little house, and tapped on the window.

"Who is there?" cried a feeble, frightened voice within. It was the voice of a sick, old, gentle woman.

"I," answered the Rabbi in a husky peasant voice, "It is I, Vasil."

"Which Vasil? What do you want Vasil?"

"I have wood to sell," answered the sham peasant. "Cheap, next to nothing."

The woman sighed and said: "My house is cold, I am ill, and I need the wood but I cannot afford to pay."

"Look, you are ill and I am willing to trust you. We have such a great and mighty God and you do not trust Him, not even for the cost of a miserable bundle of wood!"

"And who will light the stove?" groaned the widow.

"I will," said the rabbi.

While laying the wood in the stove, he repeated the first part of the *selichos* prayer. While he lighted the stove, he recited the second part of the *selichos* prayer. And when the fire was burning, he chanted the third part of the *selichos* prayer.

All this the Lithuanian saw. Later when anyone in town

6

told how the rabbi disappeared early every morning at *selichos* time, perhaps to heaven, the Lithuanian bowed his head and quietly added:

"Yes, who knows. . . . Maybe even higher than that!"

Let us realize, as did the rabbi of Nemirov, that far more important than the utterance of our lips, are the deeds to which they should prompt us.

A revealing story is told about the rabbi of the *Chasidim,* the Master of the Good Name. Once on the High Holidays he refused to enter the synagogue. When pressed for an explanation he said, "I refuse to enter because there are too many prayers in the synagogue, and not enough coming out."

Too often we carry our prayers into the synagogue. Too often we merely deposit them there and promptly forget about them. Not often enough do we emerge from the synagogue fortified with the determination to fulfill our prayers through deeds. More important than the prayers we bring into the synagogue are the prayers we carry out in our hearts and in our minds as we leave the synagogue to enter workshops in which the sincerity of our prayers is tested.

2

Rosh Hashanah Evening Service

"Bless God" (A-10; B-23; S-6)

Bor'chu is the call to worship. This call to worship has come down to us from the days when the Temple in Jerusalem was the center of our religious life. As the last rays of the setting sun faded in the darkening sky, a priest would call out from one of the towers of the Temple: *"Bor'chu es Adonoi ha-m'vorach*—Bless ye the Lord, the Blessed One." And the people, gathered in the courtyard, would respond: *"Boruch Adoni ha-m'voroch l'olom vo'ed*—Blessed be the Lord who is blessed for all eternity."

The call to bless God is the conscience within us. It calls upon us to bless God by serving Him well. The conscience calls but the choice is with man. He can, if he chooses, answer the *Bor'chu* that resounds within him by saying *Boruch*.

Conscience is man's awareness that *there is a difference between right and wrong* and that it is his duty to distinguish between them. It is the voice of the Creator urging man to live up to the divine image wihin him, to search and to strive, to hope and to pray, to discover and to apply, to work and to sacrifice for that which is right. It is the authentic voice of God speaking to man and saying, *"u'vocharto vachayim,"* choose life and make of it something beautiful, true and worthwhile. It is the inexorable universal prompting to reject that which is wrong.

However, the conscience does not tell us *what* is right and *what* is wrong. To distinguish between them is the privilege and burden of free and moral man. Our moral judgments are influenced by our creative use of reason, our experience, the facts at our disposal, circumstance, and need. But, the starting point in our effort to recognize what is right must be the starting point of this *Maariv* service—recognition of the call to worship God, and our willingness to respond to it. The acceptance and proper function of conscience can lead to an enlightened and happy conscience. Much of our woe springs from an unhappy conscience. As the talmudic rabbi, Jose ben Halafta (Berachot 7a), put it: "One pang of conscience is more painful than many lashes."

Every man is a temple in miniature. Within each of us there is felt and heard the call to worship God (*Bor'chu es Adonoy*). Many of us, however, refuse to answer, "Blessed be the Lord (*Boruch Adonoy*)." Would that every man and every home became a miniature temple dedicated to the worship of God! The whole world could become a veritable Jerusalem, a city of peace and brotherhood, if only men would answer the call to bless God.

"Blessed art Thou, O Lord, Who Brings on the Evening."
(A-11; B-23; S-6)

Primitive man feared the evening. The ancients even constructed a religion on the basis of their fear of the night. They called the darkness, the god of evil; the light they designated as the god of goodness. According to their outlook, Light and Darkness were locked in deadly conflict, each seeking supremacy over the other and over the world. Judaism, however, interpreted light and darkness as instruments of the same God. Both are part of the same divine plan; both serve the needs of man; both follow each other in logical and orderly sequence. The night, according to Judaism, was intended to bring rest and peace from the wearying tasks of the day. An object of fear became, thus, a source of blessing.

Too often, we let our fears overcome us, or we waste our strength fighting them. The more we submit to and the more we fight our fears, the deeper they invade us. Where there is fear, there is need of understanding either of ourselves or of the source of our fear. Sometimes we create our own fears; sometimes our fears are real. But they are never completely external or unrelated to us. Always the damage they do, or fail to do, depends on our interpretation of, and our reaction to them.

We fear, mostly, what we fail adequately to understand. This is true of our political and moral anxieties as well as of our physical fears. Triumphant living involves the conversion of our fears from foes into friends. And Judaism is a philosophy and a way of triumphant living. It says: "The beginning of wisdom is the fear of the Lord." Men who fear God are less inclined to fear life, its difficulties, and its dangers. Men who have faith in God fear less the eventide of life, the dark moments of the day, and the black shadows that engulf us in the final sleep.

"Blessed art Thou, O Lord, Who Loves His People Israel"
(A-11; S-6; B-23)

This is a prayer of thanksgiving to God for the love He manifested when He gave us the Torah. People generally think of themselves as blessed when they come into possession of material things. The ancients considered prosperity and military victory as evidence of their god's favor; the god's disfavor was evidenced in depression and defeat. People often looked upon suffering as a sign of divine disfavor. Part of the Christian world still considers Jewish suffering the consequence of Israel's rejection by God. From the standpoint of Judaism, however, suffering and persecution are looked upon as burdens, humbly borne by those who serve God. Jews have always been ready to make sacrifices and to endure suffering in the service of God. That is the way the children of Israel express to their Heavenly Father appreciation for the love He showed them when He bestowed upon them the Torah.

Parents concerned with the wholesome spiritual development of their children should ponder over the tremendous significance of the lesson contained in this prayer. Often we shower our children with expensive gifts as manifestations of our love for them. We are exasperated and confounded when we find that despite our beneficence they feel rejected and unloved. We are perplexed and worried when despite all we do for them they show no appreciation and little willingness to please us by living up to our expectations of them.

The key to this enigma rests in the treasure box of this prayer; it is the key that can open up the hearts of our children to our love, and make them better sons and daughters. Because the Jews received the Torah, they considered themselves loved by God. If we want our children to feel our love we must give them Torah, more spiritual guidance, persistence in and insistence on pursuits which demand disciplines and sacrifices. Then they will be more willing to strive toward the highest standards set by their elders.

"Hear O Israel, the Lord our God, the Lord is One."

(A-11; S-7; B-23)

This is one of the most important sentences in all world literature. The basis for all ethics and morals, it is the foundation upon which rests our hope that mankind will yet live in brotherhood and in peace. Faith in one God is the indispensable prerequisite for our faith in the oneness of mankind. The Prophet, Malachi, formulated that truth in the following simple words:

"Have we not all one Father?

Hath not one God created us?

11

Why then do we deal treacherously, one man against his brothers?"

The three paragraphs of the *Shema* are taken from the Torah. They speak primarily of the sources of motivation for optimal behavior. Our conduct as individuals and as a people should be rooted in the following mainsprings of ethical vigor and integrity:

1. Love of God: *"Thou shalt Love the Lord, thy God."* (Deut. 6:4-9) (A-11; S-7; B-23)

This implies a desire to please God and to conduct ourselves according to His will. We should make the pleasure of God the object of our life. We would do well to ask ourselves as often as possible, "What doth the Lord require of me?" Too often our conduct is determined by the question, "What do I want?" The earliest education of our children should instill in their hearts and minds the desire to build their lives according to God's will rather than on their natural selfishness. Of course, too often we assume that our will is God's will and attribute divine approval to our own self-centered desires or opinions. We are only human and cannot be perfect but we are on the right track when we stop to ask ourselves, "What does God expect me to do?"

2. Fear of God: *"Take heed to yourselves lest . . . the displeasure of the Lord be kindled against you."* (Deut. 11:13-21) (A-12; S-8; B-24)

This implies that we need knowledge of the consequences that flow from the violation of God's law. We teach our children the danger of fire because we want them to be physically safe. Why not teach them the danger of conduct that consumes us morally and spiritually? Why not help them recognize that man invites destruction when he kindles the displeasure of God. Fear of God is perhaps an unfortunate term. We do not want our children to fear God but to fear offending Him. The Hebrew term for fear is *"Yirah."* Its root word really means to see, to be cognizant of the ever-present God, to be aware that He sees us. "The beginning of wisdom is *"Yiras Elohim,"* the consciousness that our conduct counts because we are constantly in the presence of God who sees us and, with love, watches over us.

3. Free Will *"That you may look upon it and remember the commandments of the Lord and do them."* (Numbers 15: 37-41)   (A-12; S-8; B-24)

This is a cardinal principle of Judaism. "Everything is in the hands of God except our decision to accept Him and to live according to His will." Our Rabbis used to say, "If thou hast done God's will against thine own will, then thou hast done only His will." The goal of all moral education is to help man accept God's will as his will. We are free to choose but the proper exercise of freedom is to choose that which is right. In his quest for the right, man is not wholly unaided. The Torah and God stand ready to help him choose and find the way to righteousness, but the decision rests with him. In order to provide our children with adequate moral preparation for life, we need to give them Torah and God, moral instruction and spiritual faith. The ultimate decision will be in their hands for the Creator has endowed them, too, with the privilege and responsibility of free will.

"Blessed art Thou, O Lord, Redeemer of Israel."
(A-13; S-9; B-27)

History is more than the story of man's effort. There are aspects of history that can be explained only in terms of coincidence and accident, or in terms of the power and purpose of God. The historical experience of Israel led it to the conclusion that its survival could not be explained in terms of coincidence or accident, but rather in terms of a God who "redeems us from all tyrants and saves us from the hands of all oppressors." Was it an accident that saved us from the enslavement in Egypt? Was it merely by chance that we outlived a long parade of marching world conquerors who sought, but failed, to absorb us? Has it been by our own power that we escaped the grave dug for us by empires and nations mightier than we? Our experience has led us to conclude that man oppresses and enslaves, but God ransoms and redeems. "He has maintained us in life and has not suffered our foot to slip. He has caused us to surmount our enemies and has raised our strength above all who hated us."

This conception of history is a logical, empirical conclusion based on past experience. It is also a matter of faith with us as we face the future. With this faith we shall cleave the waters of any new Red Seas that must be opened to freedom. This is the kind of faith with which we must imbue ourselves and which we must give to our children as an everlasting inheritance. Faith in God as the Redeemer is a good faith.

"Blow ye the trumpet on the new moon, in the time appointed, on our solemn feast day. For it is a statute for Israel, an ordinance of the God of Jacob." (Psalm 81: 4-5)

(A-14; S-10; B-29)

We are told that Moses spent forty days on Mt. Sinai preparing the Law. Then he descended with the tablets of stone on which were inscribed the Ten Commandments. When he came into camp, he found the people worshipping a golden calf. In a fit of anger he broke the tablets, ground the golden calf to dust, reproached the people, and punished the sinners. He instructed the people in the worship of the true God and led them in prayers of repentance. On the new moon of Elul, The Holy One, blessed be He, said to Moses: "Come up into the Mount" (Exodus 24:12). Then a ram's horn was blown throughout the camp, for behold, Moses was ascending Mt. Sinai. With him ascended the hopes and prayers of the people that God might forgive them and that they might not stray

14

again. Forty days later on the tenth of Tishre, the Day of Atonement, Moses returned with a new set of tablets and assurance of forgiveness. Therefore, the sages instituted the custom of blowing the ram's horn daily except on Sabbaths from the first day of the Hebrew month of Elul for the forty day period ending at the conclusion of the Day of Atonement. Generally, the *Shofar* is blown at the end of the daily morning service. In some places it is blown at the afternoon service as well. In still other places the horn is blown at the evening service. According to some rituals, the horn is blown at this point of the service on the evening of Rosh Hashanah. In our ritual, reference is made to the blowing, but the horn is not sounded.

AMIDAH   (A-15; S-11; B-31)

Amidah means "standing." This part of the service is called *Amidah* because we say it in a standing position. As we utter the prayers contained in the *Amidah,* we should feel that we are standing in the very presence of God. Therefore, as a gesture of reverence, it is customary before the beginning and ending of this part of the service, to step back three paces, then to step forward three paces, and to bow before the Lord.

The *Amidah* consists of 7 prayers. Each prayer ends with the blessing of thanksgiving to God.

1. *"Blessed art Thou, Shield of Abraham."*
                                              (A-15; S-11; B-31)

Just as God was the shield of Abraham so has he been the protector of the seed of Abraham throughout the ages. The Jewish doctrine of the "merit of the fathers," teaches that every generation benefits from the spiritual heritage bequeathed unto it by past generations. We are the beneficiaries of the virtues of Abraham, Isaac and Jacob, the founding fathers of our people and our faith. Their sacrifices and spiritual achievements enrich our lives. However, it is not enough to live on

15

our spiritual heritage. If our faith is to be a shield unto us and unto generations yet to come, we, like our forefathers, must be prepared to meet our duties to God and to the moral and spiritual challenges of our times. When we live in accordance with the spiritual heritage of our ancestors, the virtue of which we are capable is strengthened, our lives are rendered more significant, and we add to the growing heritage that it is our duty to pass on to the next generation. If we want our children to live happily, usefully, and meaningfully as Jews, then we, too, must live Jewishly. As parents, it is our responsibility and privilege to bequeath to our children a shield of faith that will protect them spiritually.

2. *"Blessed art Thou Who givest life to the dead."*
(A-15; S-11; B-31)

He awakens the dead to new life. Life, the product of the Creator, never ends. We shed the body, whose life is temporary, to enter into the eternal life of the soul. We leave our earthly abode to go to the *beth olam,* the eternal home.

The Torah, which is a blueprint for human conduct in this life, makes no direct reference to life after death, but in the writings of the rabbis there are many references to the Hereafter. The classic statement in the "Ethics of the Fathers," expresses the rabbinic view: "This world is like a vestibule to the World to Come. Prepare yourself in this antechamber that you may enter the main hall."

It is not easy to believe in a Hereafter. Many people even doubt the reality and significance of *this* life. How then can we believe that this life is intended as preparation for a new life? Yet, the Hereafter gives the Here meaning. The assurance of continuity gives purpose to the contemporary. The contemplation of a future gives man direction and interest in the present. Can it be that all our moral and spiritual effort in this world has no meaning beyond the grave?

We have a choice between believing that this life is prepa-

ration or that this life is all there is, and there is no proof
for either. Let us, then, choose the belief that strengthens.
Once, a rabbi heard one of his disciples reciting the "Thirteen
Principles of Jewish Faith." The disciple began, "I believe
with a perfect faith," and then interrupted himself with, "I
don't understand it, I don't understand it." "What is it that
you don't understand?" asked the rabbi. "I say that I believe,
but if I really believe, then how can I possibly doubt?" asked
the disciple. "And if I do not believe, why am I telling myself
lies?"

"Do not be concerned, my son," said the rabbi. "It means
that the words, 'I believe,' are a prayer. What you are really
saying is 'O, that I may believe',." Whereupon the disciple
exclaimed with joy, "That I may believe, Lord of the World!
O, that I may believe!"

We, like the disciple, should pray for the strength to believe,
for it is a belief that strengthens.

Our ancestors observed that in nature there is no death.
What seems like death in nature is merely the interlude between
life and revival. Death is the winter between the fall and
spring of life. Just as God wondrously awakes to life the seed,
slumbering in the soil, so God stirs the dead sleeping in the
earth to new life. In death we shed our tired bodies in order
to come back to new and stronger life. We cannot know the
mystery of life beyond the grave but if there is a God, then the
grave cannot be the end. An ancient rabbi put it this way: "If
the creator could make something that lives (man) out of
something inert or lifeless (earth), then surely he can restore
to life that which already had life in it."

3. *"Blessed art Thou the Holy King."*

(A-16; S-12; B-33)

Something about rare *beauty* arouses in us a feeling of
deep joy. Something about a startling discovery of *truth* stimu-
lates in us a sense of power. Something about a sincere act of

17

righteousness quickens our faith and brightens our outlook. Good music stirs us to ecstacy, fine art to contentment, the pageantry of the skies to awe, the endless cycles of dynamic creation to reverence. Combine all these feelings into one to approximate the mood that enthralls and overwhelms man when he is really aware of coming into the presence of God. It is called "holiness." It means something different, apart, out of the world, somewhat beyond our keenest intellect and most exquisitely sensitive imaginings. When we invite God into our homes and hearts and really dedicate them to His service, we are sometimes privileged to experience this feeling of holiness. Art tries to capture the structure and the moods of the universe; science analyzes the substances that go into the structure, and the laws that govern its movements. Both capture only fleeting aspects, never the whole. Only through real religion, complete dedication to God through all the senses, all the mind, and emotion, can we feel the essence of it all, God's holiness.

4. *"Blessed art Thou . . . Who hallowest Israel and the day of remembrance, Rosh Hashanah."*

(A-17; S-13; B-36)

Israel has been hallowed by the Torah. Observance of the Torah, of the commandments and ceremonies, of the ethical and ritual duties prescribed in it, makes us God-conscious. It is difficult to describe the holy joy that pervades the humblest Jewish home in which the rites of Judaism are devoutly observed. Just as love can be felt only by those who love, so holiness can be felt only by those who are engaged in the practice of holy rite. We should resolve to bring this holiness into our homes.

On this Day of Remembrance, one of the holiest days of the year, we should resolve to train ourselves through Israel's holy rite to come into and feel the presence of the Holy One.

5. *"Blessed art Thou who restorest His Divine Presence unto Zion."*   (A-18; S-14; B-37)

We pray that God return to Zion but we are preoccupied by the tremendous task of bringing back to Israel the dispossessed and homeless. It would be absurd to pray for the return of God to Zion without supporting the present effort to accomplish the return of the people. But it is equally absurd to bring the people back without supporting the prayer that God return to Zion. When the Jewish people and God meet in the Holy Land, Torah will once more issue from Zion and His holy word from Jerusalem. In order that Israel may become the world spiritual fortress it once was, we must support and enlarge its Torah institutions and build new ones in the Holy Land.

The Temple in Jerusalem was built by King Solomon about 925 B.C.E. and destroyed by the Babylonians in 586 B.C.E. It was rebuilt in 516 B.C.E. and was destroyed again by the Romans in 70 C.E. Since it had been the center of a dynamic and creative Judaism, its destruction was a great blow to the spirit of our people. Among other things, it marked the end of the last tangible evidence of their independence. They never ceased, therefore, to pray for the restoration of the Temple and its Service.

The independence of the Jewish people, of Israel, has been achieved. The next step is the establishment of a new temple, a great religious center in Jerusalem, which will serve as a symbol that Jews interpret independence and freedom as apportunities for the worship of God.

Torah once came forth from Zion. We pray that it may again be the privilege of the Jewish people to bring forth from Zion lessons that will strengthen the moral and spiritual fibre of the whole world.

19

6. *"Blessed art Thou to Whom it is a joy to give thanks."*
(A-18; S-14; B-37)

It is essential to our well-being that we be equally conscious of our needs and of our possessions. It is important to appreciate the blessings that enrich our lives. Without appreciation, there is no enrichment. We do not really possess and enjoy that which we take for granted. Man's happiness does not depend so much on *how much he has,* but rather on *how much he appreciates what he has.* The key to happiness is gratitude.

The rabbis, is order to encourage in us a sense of gratitude, instructed us to say at least one hundred blessings of thanksgiving every day. "He is rich," taught the rabbis, "who is content with his portion."

I shall never forget the young army doctor dying in my arms who asked me to pray that he might live until his family could arrive at his bedside. Only a miracle helped him do so. After greeting and comforting them, he died with a prayer of thanksgiving and a smile. He had asked for so little yet, because he appreciated those few extra hours more than some of us appreciate a whole lifetime, he died happy.

7. *"Blessed art Thou who blesses His people with peace."*
(A-18; S-14; B-37)

Appropriately, the final blessings of the *Amidah* is always the prayer for peace. When men and nations recognize that "the earth is the Lord's," and are truly grateful for the blessings he gives to us all, they will act toward each other with the charity and humility that make for increased humanity and peace. Real and lasting peace has its roots in grateful acknowledgement that God gives us blessings to enjoy and to share with our fellow men.

"IT IS OUR DUTY"

(A-22; S-22; B-43)

This prayer consists of two sections. The first is a proclamation of Israel's worship of the One God. It protests both the immanent conception of God that identifies Him only with the earth and the transcendentalist conception that sees Him exclusively as the God of Heaven. In Judaism, the God of Heaven and Earth is One.

The second section is a reaffirmation of the essential Jewish belief that humanity will be one when all men come to recognize that God is One. The brotherhood of man is inherent in the Fatherhood of God.

"The Mourner's Kaddish"

(A-22; S-23; B-45)

Originally, the *Kaddish* was a prayer for the speedy establishment of God's kingdom on earth. This *Kaddish* was recited at the conclusion of each section of the service, and at the completion of the entire service. Subsequently it became a practice to recite this prayer at the conclusion of a period of group study. The rabbis reasoned that the study of Torah leads to good deeds thereby advancing the coming of the Kingdom of Righteousness.

The *Kaddish* is our prayer for the speedy establishment of God's Kingdom on earth. Originally it was recited at the conclusion of a discourse or a period of group study. The rabbis reasoned that the study of Torah leads to good deeds thereby advancing the coming of the Kingdom. They therefore considered the *Kaddish* an appropriate concluding prayer. In time, the doxology passed from the school to the synagogue where it was recited also at the completion of distinct section of the prayer service and at the end of the entire service. The rabbis felt that prayer, like study, brings men closer to the good life. At a later time it became customary for disciples to recite a special *Kaddish* in tribute to a great master of the Law when he died. A scholar's life, they reasoned, is like a lesson in the Law. Finally, the democratic impulse in the Jewish people led to the decision that the same honor should be extended to all the departed. They felt that every

21

man during his lifetime performs some good deeds that promote the establishment of the Kingdom of God on earth.

There are four different *Kaddeshim*.

Kaddish of the Rabbis—Said at the end of the reading of a lesson from the Torah or the Talmud.

Half *Kaddish*—said at conclusion of each section of a service.

Full *Kaddish*—said at the end of a complete service.

Kaddish of the Orphon—said at certain intervals by the mourners.

Kaddish, like the *Borchu, Kedusha* and other prayers dwelling on the holiness of God, may be recited only when a quorum of at least ten adult males is present (*Minyan*). According to rabbinic thought, the *Shechinah* (Divine Presence) is in the midst of the community. The larger the community engaged in His worship, the greater the impact of His revelation. The rabbis felt very strongly that progress toward the highest ideals and the achievement of holiness in the world were dependent on community effort rather than on the limited resources of the individual. The self can be fully realized only in a society; similarly, the individual can discharge all his duties to God completely, only in collaboration with the community. Man's search for God may lead to neglect of the world rather than to its improvement unless he makes that search in, and with, a community. The phenomenon of moral man in an immoral society attests to the greatness of human personality. However, the quality of life is improved and its significance enhanced only to the extent that moral man contributes to or bands together to transform, in a collective effort, the nature of our society. The individual dies but the community endures and conserves the values which would otherwise die with the individual. "Do not separate yourself from the community," is a frequent admonition of the sages. Should the individual be prevented from attending a congregational service, he is urged to say his prayers at the time set for community prayers so he can identify himself with the group, in spirit if not in flesh. *Tefillah b'tsibbur,* the preference of congregational or community prayer over individual worship, was emphatically endorsed by the sages.

However, the importance of the individual was not minimized either. One life is as important as the life of the entire world. Being social and spiritual realists, the sages recognized that isolated individuals, withdrawn from the community, cannot achieve the sanctification of God's name in the world nor can they improve the moral quality of the community and the social order.

"EXTOLLED"

(A-23; S-25; B-56)

The author of this liturgical poem was the Jewish *Dayan* (Judge) Daniel Ben Judah who lived in Rome about 1300. The poem is based on the thirteen principles of Jewish faith as formulated by the Medieval philosopher of Judaism, Moses Maimonides (b. 1135-d. 1204).

Judaism is, at least in part, a system of spiritual concepts (beliefs), moral convictions (laws), and religious practices (ritual). The moral laws and ritual practices have been carefully defined, codified, and endowed with authority. Not so the spiritual beliefs. Although there have been many attempts to formulate and to define authoritively the basic beliefs of Judaism, no such formulation enjoys universal acceptance. While, traditionally, there was almost complete agreement on what was required of a Jew in terms of "deed," no such agreement ever existed on what was required in terms of "creed."

Down through the ages individual prophets and sages have attempted to formulate the basic beliefs of Judaism. Maimonides gave us thirteen principles of Jewish faith that constitute the content of the *"Yigdal."*

1. God is the Creator of the universe.
2. There is only one God.

23

3. God has no bodily form nor is He a force contained within a body.

4. God always was, and He always will be.

5. Only God is worthy of our worship.

6. God has endowed some men with prophecy, extraordinary moral and intellectual powers by which they have been able to attain to a degree of truth and a quality of knowledge beyond the capacity of others.

7. God endowed Moses with the power of prophecy and made him the greatest of all prophets.

8. God revealed to Moses the Torah and the hermeneutical principles for the application of His Laws to meet the needs of changing and growing society.

9. The Law of God as contained in the Torah is perfect, complete and final. Nothing may be added to or subtracted from it.

10. God knows the thoughts and deeds of man; the Creator knows his creature.

11. God rewards those who choose to keep His commandments and disciplines those who transgress them.

12. God will send a Messiah from the descendents of King David. The Messiah will be endowed with extraordinary wisdom and power to establish God's kingdom on earth.

13. God will redeem the living and restore the dead to life.

These thirteen principles may be divided, logically, into three groups dealing with the three major assumptions of Jewish Theology:

1. Existence of God (Principles 1-5)
2. Revelation (Principles 6-9)
3. The Moral Order of the World (Principles 10-13)

The first set of assumptions is a description of the Deity. No attempt is made to prove his existence.

Once, an unbeliever came to Rabbi Akiba and asked him who created the world. When Rabbi Akiba answered that God was the Creator, the unbeliever demanded proof. Whereupon, Rabbi Akiba pointed to the man's coat and said, "Who made that?" Why, a weaver of course," replied the unbeliever. "Before I can believe you, I must have proof," said the rabbi. "Why should I give you proof," said the man impatiently, "this coat couldn't have made itself." The kindly rabbi then said to the unbeliever, "Do you not also know that God created the world? Just as the house must have its builder, and a coat its weaver, so the world points to the Holy One as its Creator."

The world is either the result of a blind *accident* or a deliberate act of *creation.* Life is either the chance evolution of an atom, or the premeditated, well-planned, purposive achievement of a God capable of contemplating and fulfilling His will.

Intuitively, the Jewish mind has always understood life in terms of God rather than blind power, as a product rather than an accident, as creation rather than chance. It wasn't until Judaism came in contact with Greek philosophy that the teachers of our religion began to formulate proofs for the existence of God. By experience and reason we can find and construct proofs for the belief in God. In the last analysis, though, the belief in God is a matter of faith, a conviction that comes to us through our power of intuition rather than our powers of observation and reason. Thus, there is room for some degree of agnosticism in our approach to God. Since we really cannot *know,* we are justified in saying, "We do not know."

We all build our lives on a foundation of basic, reasonable assumptions and beliefs. We may not always be able to control the objective, demonstrable factors of our life structure, but we can and should select very discriminatingly our beliefs. If a belief is intellectually reasonable, morally advisable, psychologically uplifting, spiritually edifying, then that belief is an assumption of which to order our lives. The basic assumption of which Judaism has been built and Jewish life sustained is the belief in God.

The second group of Maimonides' principles (verses 6-9) deals with revelation. By revelation, we mean that God reveals His will to man. God does reveal His will to those who seek him in truth. Nevertheless, even nature, which is only part of the will of God, keeps some secrets from her most assiduous student, the scientist. Sometimes, the more mysteries he solves, the more he creates. How much more is this true of our understanding of God? The more we contemplate on the meaning of God, the more mysteries we uncover. Only the naive say that there is no mystery. Ignorance is either the insistence that all is known or knowable, or the profession that nothing is known and all is mystery. Life has both mystery and meaning. Through communication with God, or revelation, we extract a little more meaning from mystery. Since God is infinite, His mystery is inexhaustible and His revelations to us will always continue.

The third set of principles, verse 10 and 11, deals with ethics, with reward and punishment, or the moral order of the universe. Maimonides makes a cardinal principle of the conviction that our conduct counts, i.e., God takes cognizance of every thought and every deed of man.

The last section, verses 12 and 13, deals with the future that God has in store for us, the coming of the Messiah and the ultimate resurrection of the dead.

The sages of Israel considered the salvation of the individual Jew as indissolubly linked with the salvation of the whole house of Israel, and the salvation of Israel as connected with the triumph of righteousness in the world. The future age of victory for righteousness and peace is called the Messianic Age. The Messianic Age of universal justice and peace will not be the product solely of man's efforts. God will send a *messiah* (anointed one) to restore the scattered children of Israel to the land of Israel. Unlike the messiah of Christianity who is thought of as the son of God, or God himself, the Jewish messiah is a mortal man of the seed of David. Unlike the Christian messiah who died to wash away the sins of all men, the Jewish messiah will live to guide the world to virtue by establishing peace and justice, and the universal worship of the one God. From the standpoint of Judaism, the messiah is not God. Every man has messiah, the promise of redemption, within him. The grace of God will fulfill it.

These are the thirteen principles of Maimonides' *Code of Jewish Creed,* the basic beliefs of traditional Judaism. We recite them daily in our morning service. As we joyously sing the beliefs of our ancestors we ought to reflect that upon us rests the obligation to discover what we of the twentieth century can, and should, believe.

THE NEW YEAR GREETING

The Hebrew word *"tovah"* means "good," and the translation, "happy," is not correct. The basis of our Rosh Hashanah prayers is the hope for *goodness* rather than for personal happiness. Happiness is something that you or I feel, personally, within ourselves. *Goodness* is a more mature concept of human experience. It extends beyond the horizons of our personal life and reaches out into the lives of others.

The earliest concept of goodness known to man is found in the first chapter of the Bible. It originates with God himself. God looked out and saw a world that was "void and without form, and darkness was upon the face of the deep." God did not want the world to be dark and void. Therefore He called out, "Let there be light." And there was light. Suddenly a world that was dark and formless, ugly and chaotic, began to assume a pattern of contrast and order, life and meaning. What did God say when He saw all this? Did he speak in terms of happiness? Not at all. The Bible says "And God saw that it was good *(tov)*." God had created something worthwhile and He pronounced it good *(tov)*. The joy of working, the joy of creating, is the real *good* that brings happiness.

Herein lies the interpretationof *"shanah tovah,"* a *good*

27

year. A New Year can be a *shanah tovah* only if it results in the creation of something good, something worthwhile, something that benefits not only ourselves but others as well. When we turn to our neighbor and wish him a *"shanah tovah,"* we wish him much more than food and drink and laughter. We wish our neighbor the priceless joy of doing something worthwhile in the New Year, something that will enable him to look back after the year is gone and say, "It has been a *shanah tovah* —a good year." If a man can say the year has been a good one it will have brought him happiness.

When we are young we are taught the importance of *being* good. But Rosh Hashanah tells us it is not enough merely to *be* good. We must *do* good. "May you be inscribed for a good year" is a joyful reminder that we must resolve to do good, not only for ourselves, but for others. In keeping such a resolution we shall be living up to the highest ideals of Judaism.

"May you be inscribed for a good year," is not just a greeting, it is a blessing. There is a vast difference between a greeting and a blessing. A greeting does not imply any particular responsibility on the part of the well wisher—a blessing does. When the priests in the Temple blessed the people, they raised their hands to symbolize that when we bless our fellows we must be prepared to lift a helping hand. When we wish our neighbors and friends a good year we, too, must be prepared to *help* make it a good year.

28

3

Rosh Hashanah Morning Service

PART ONE

BLESSINGS OF THE DAWN
(A-25 to 62; B-51 to 89; S-26 to 42)

The first part of the morning Service is called "Blessings of the Dawn." The observant Jew starts the day with a blessing and ends it with a prayer of thanksgiving. This is much better than starting the day with an imprecation and ending it with a sense of futility. A good remedy for morning grouchiness and evening fatigue is the tonic of prayer; the cultivation of a wholesome habit of greeting and saying farewell to a day of life with a *brocho* (blessing).

According to *Mesichta Menachot* (Talmudic Tractate "Meal Offerings"), a Jew is required to recite a minimum of 100 blessings of thanksgiving every day. The rabbis wanted every day to be Thanksgiving Day. They felt that there are at least 100 things for which man should thank God daily. The worst form of spiritual poverty and the cause of most unhappiness is our failure to be conscious of the many blessings that surround us every moment of the day. In order that we may be aware of these blessings and draw the happiness that they should bring into our lives, we are enjoined by our religion to cultivate the habit and the attitude of thanksgiving.

29

In *Mesichta Brochot* (Talmudic Tractate "Blessings") the sages tell us:

⌄ "When a man is given a cup (of wine) and does not say the appropriate blessing, he shortens his days." What remarkable insight! The man who drinks from the cup of life and does not feel prompted to thank God shortchanges himself of life's deepest dimension—the feeling of blessing. Only when we are conscious of and grateful for our blessings, can we really enjoy the feeling of being blessed.

The *Birchas Hashachar* section of our service instructs us also, that every day affords us opportunity to find, to fashion, and to add new temporal blessings with which to enrich life and add to human happiness.

At the dawn of Jewish time it was told to Abraham, the founding father of our people and of our faith, that the goal of all his strivings should be to make his life a source of blessing to Jewish generations yet unborn and to all the families of the earth. Should anyone ask what the aim of life is, let the Jew answer, "to be grateful for God's blessings, to enjoy them prudently, to share them charitably, and to increase blessing in the land."

"In Thine Abundant Love, I Enter Thy House."

(A-25; B-51; S-26)

This prayer is said when we enter the synagogue. Coming to the synagogue is spoken of today as a duty. That is very fine. Would that all Jews regarded synagogue attendance as obligatory! However, we should really regard synagogue attendance as a privilege if we are to derive the full value that is inherent in the experience of coming into the House of God.

The synagogue is not the only House of God. The church, the mosque, the temple—the whole world is the House of God. He is our Host and we are His guests. It is because He loves His children that He invites us to enjoy His hospitality and to partake of His bounty. If men would only remember that

30

they are God's guests in this world and that the food they eat, the air they breathe, the bounty they enjoy are God's gifts of love to man, they would surely live more lovingly, more graciously and more gratefully.

When the Jew says this prayer in the synagogue: "Lord, I love the habitation of Thy house," he is saying, "Lord, I love life which Thou givest me in Thine abundant love." Love of life as a divine gift is the spirit that has forged the miracle of Jewish survival and has given us the will to carry bravely the yoke of commandment and obligation. This prayer is an affirmation of the value of life and of our gratitude for it.

"And commanded us to wrap ourselves in the fringed garment."
(A-35; B-53; S-26)

In ancient times a garment made of a single square piece of woolen cloth was worn. Among the Hebrews, this outer garment was called a *talis.* There was, originally, nothing distinctive about the *talis.* It was much like the outer robe worn by many other oriental peoples and like the toga worn by the Romans. However, one thing eventually made the *talis* more than a mere garment: *tzitzis,* or special fringes. The fourth book of the Bible, Numbers 15:37-41, prescribes the wearing of special fringes, *tzitzis,* on the four corners of the garment. The commandment to wear *tzitzis* and the reason for doing so are given to us in the following words of the Torah:

"And the Lord spoke unto Moses, saying, "Speak unto the children of Israel, and bid them that they make them throughout their generations fringes in the corners of their garments, and that they put with the fringe of each corner a thread of blue. And it shall be unto you for a fringe, that you may look upon it, and remember all the commandments of the Lord, and do them; and that ye go not about your own heart and your own eyes, after which ye are wont to go astray; that ye may remember and do all My commandments, and be Holy unto your God."

31

By obeying this commandment, the Jew carries with him a constant reminder that his conduct must be based not only on his own desires, but on the laws of the Torah; that his heart and his eyes are not the final judge of right and wrong; that conscience and sense of duty to God must determine his actions; and that the best way to sanctify life is to observe the laws and teachings of the Torah.

The four corners of the *talis* are interpreted to represent the four corners of the earth and to impress upon the Jewish consciousness that the laws of justice apply equally to all peoples in every part of the world.

The use of the thread of blue is explained thus in the Talmud:

"Because blue resembles the sea, the sea resembles the sky, and the sky resembles the Chair of Glory or the Throne of God." The art of dyeing threads sky-blue was a secret of the Jews of the city of Acre. After the land was destroyed and the people dispersed, the special technique was forgotten and the use of the thread of blue was discontinued.

In the course of time, Jews living in different lands adopted the garb of their fellow countrymen and the practice of wearing *tzitzis* in the corners of their outer garments came to an end. The commandment of the Torah was, however, not violated. In place of the old practice, two new practices emerged. First, the *talis* was made smaller and its use was restricted to the synagogue. At the beginning of the morning service the Jew kisses the fringes of his *talis* and pronounces a benediction as he wraps it around his shoulders. Second, in order to fulfil the biblical injunction to wear fringes at all times, a *talis katan* (small *talis*) was devised. This small *talis* is called *arba kanfos* (four corners). It is a rectangular piece of cloth with *tzitzis* in its four corners and an opening in the center to enable it to pass over the head to rest on the shoulders. It is worn under the outer garments by every pious male from earliest childhood. To this day, the use of the *talis* and of the *talis katan* are helpful means of impressing upon the child that he walks always in the presence of God and owes allegiance to God's Law. The *talis* serves, to those who appreciate its meaning and employ its use, as an instrument of faith. Above all, its purpose is to protect us against a fallacy in human thinking and conduct which divorces religion from our daily activities. Its purpose is to make us deeply conscious that whether we work or play, during every moment of wakefulness, we must not forget God.

"How precious is Thy loving kindness. The children of man take refuge under the protection of Thy sheltering care."

The fringes (*tzitzis*) are reminders of the 613 Commandments of the Torah. When we wrap the *talis* over the head and shoulders, we express in ritual the idea that we submit to God's laws and we come under His loving care and protection. A feeling of security is generated by the observance of the *mitzvos,* by the fulfillment of our duties to God. Would that men were willing to spread the *talis* over the entire world! It should be obvious that we can expect the security of the spiritual life only insofar as we respect the laws designed for our spiritual protection.

Often we interpret security in terms of economic plenty. Materialist philosophies have done incalculable harm to men by fostering this mistaken notion. The satisfaction of our economic needs is only one aspect of our security and not even the most important one. What we have inside of us spiritually, and not the external environment, ultimately determines whether we have the strength necessary to meet the challenges of life. For example, parents may clothe and feed their children well and provide them adequately with all the physical necessities of life. But if they fail to equip them with the free and abundant richness of ideals, values and faith, they leave their children exposed to the deadly disease of insecurity. We want our children to be safe, to have more and to be better off than we. The result too often is the very opposite of what we want

33

really to achieve for them. Reared in an atmosphere of over-concern for their physical comfort, they do not know how to stand up under hardship. Reared in emotional overdependence, they cannot face responsibility. Reared in coddled security, they fall to pieces in a crisis. Reared in a home which overempha-sizes the importance of the material, they lack the inner spir-itual security to face life as it really is.

From the standpoint of Judaism, the purpose of education is not to make our children "better off" but better men and women, morally and spiritually. The function of education in the home and in the school is to equip them with the faith, confidence, moral conviction, ideals and values that bring them under the sheltering protection of God. Only with God in their hearts can our sons and daughters be secure. Let us give them what they really need for security.

"AT THE DAWN I SEEK THEE"

A student once interrupted his worship at this point of the service and turned to his rabbi: "Tell me, my teacher," he asked, "is not the whole world full of God's glory? Why then do I have to seek Him?" Whereupon the rabbi replied, "God dwells everywhere but man finds Him only where he seeks Him."

A story is told about a merchant who came to his rabbi to complain about another merchant who had opened a shop right next door to him. "You seem to think," said the rabbi, "that it is your shop that supports you, and you set your heart upon it instead of on God, who is your support. Set your heart on God and there will be support for both you and your rival." "But where can I find this God who will support us both?" asked the merchant. The rabbi replied: "It is written, 'Love thy neighbor as thyself, I am the Lord.' This means you should want for your neighbor what you want for yourself— and therein you will find God." From early dawn till late at night men seek a livelihood. Consequently neighbors are regarded as rivals and opponents. If, instead, we spent more time seeking God through love of fellow-man, we might have less livelihood but we would all surely have more of the real supports of life—peace, security and justice. This is true of the individual man and also of society as a whole. In this spirit, would that all men and nations might say, "At the dawn I seek Thee."

A story is told about a minister, a priest, and a rabbi who were very close companions. One day the priest said to his friends, "Sometimes I wish we were of the same religion." The minister nodded in agreement. The rabbi remarked: "Indeed, we *are* of one religion, for those who love are of one religion. Would that all religious groups sought God in the spirit of brotherhood and love. A new and brighter dawn will come upon the world when God is sought in this spirit."

FIVE BLESSINGS

(A-27; B-57; S-28)

The Hebrew word for blessing is *"brocho."* A blessing generally begins with the word *"boruch."* Here we have five blessings:

1. *The blessing for washing hands.* We thank God for having commanded us to keep our hands clean and to observe the laws of hygiene. From the standpoint of Judaism, every time we eat we are guests at God's table and every time we pray we come into His presence. Therefore, it is necessary to wash in order to appear before Him in purity. As we start our day's work in the vineyard of the Lord to toil with Him for a better world, we wash our hands and pronounce the proper benediction. This emphasis on physical cleanliness had a great deal to do with the high health standards maintained by Jews throughout the ages.

2. *A blessing in which we thank God, the Creator of the body and the Healer of all flesh.*

The God who created the heavenly bodies also created the human body. Just as he looks after the bodies in the skies so that they operate with clock-like precision and regularity so does he care for the delicate mechanisms of the human body. Because we are free to either aid God in His care of the body or to neglect and ruin it, we have responsibility for our own health. In the final analysis, however, He is the Creator and He is the Healer. The attitude of gratitude for the body, the appreciation of its complexity, the belief in its divine origin, and faith in God as the Healer are of tremendous therapeutic value.

3. *Blessed art Thou . . . to study the words of the Torah.*
4. *Blessed art Thou . . . Who gave us the Torah.*

We thank God for having given the Torah to our ancestors; pray that we too may learn and know the Torah; and hope that our descendants will continue to study and discover Torah. Torah is God's law. It is also a synonym for the continuing process of Jewish creative thinking in the moral and spiritual as well as in the cultural realm. The order of these two blessings is very revealing. One would think that the order ought to be reversed. God gave us the Torah before we were obliged to study it. The order of the blessings is intended to tell us that the Torah is not really ours until we study it and that God reveals the laws of life to us only after we make the effort to learn them.

From the standpoint of Judaism, "Cleanliness *is* Godliness." The Bible, the Talmud, and other great texts of Jewish religious law are, in a sense, treatises on cleanliness of the body, of the mind and of the soul. The purpose of Jewish Law is to combat the impurities that threaten to invade man and to protect him from unclean speech, sordid thoughts, ugly motives, impure family life and other vices that blemish our society.

The prayers here follow the logical order of the Torah. In the Book of Numbers, the discourses on the diseases of the body and the laws of physical purity precede the discussion of moral uncleanliness and the laws of spiritual holiness. *"Mens sana in corpore sano,"* was an old principle of early Judaism.

A healthy body, a healthy mind and a healthy soul are the ultimate goals of Judaism. The effort to achieve these goals for, and by, all mankind is the true worship of God.

5. *"The Lord bless thee."*

After the blessing in which we give thanks for the Torah, what is more appropriate than a blessing from the Torah? The section that follows is the Priestly Blessing from the Book of Numbers 6:24-26:

"The Lord bless thee and keep thee. The Lord make His Spirit to shine upon thee and be gracious unto thee. The Lord manifest His Presence unto thee and give thee peace."

"THESE ARE THE COMMANDMENTS"

(A-28; B-59; S-29)

Then follows a section from the Mishnah (part of the Talmud) which tells us how we can achieve the Priestly Blessing in our lives.

Mishnah Peah I declares:

"These are the commandments for which no fixed measure is imposed: leaving the corners of the field for the poor, the gift of the first fruits, the pilgrimage offering at the sanctuary on the three festivals, deeds of loving kindness and the study of the Torah. These are the commandments, the fruits of which a man enjoys in this life while the principle endures to all eternity: honoring one's father and mother, performing deeds of loving kindness, atetnding the house of study morning and evening, hospitality to wayfarers, visiting the sick, dowering the bride, accompanying the dead to the grave, devotion in prayer and making peace between man and his fellow; but the study of the Torah is equivalent to them all."

"My God I thank Thee for the soul which Thou hast given me." (A-28; B-59; S-29)

Just as God gave us a body, an outer garment of flesh, so has He given us a soul, an inner content of moral, spiritual,

37

intellectual and aesthetic quality. Is it possible to explain man's courage, vision, imagination, intellect and creative powers in terms of mere physio-chemical reactions? Surely there is more to man than the body. We can produce artificial kidneys, hearts, lungs, etc. but we cannot produce a single man who is able to think, envision, dream, fight and create. We can produce machines but not men. The quality that distinguishes man is the soul.

We do not know much about the soul. It is one of the mysteries that will forever elude man's limited comprehension. However, we believe that it is not merely a function of the body. It is, as the Hebrew expresses it, "the breath of life." The body does not give life and meaning to the soul. The soul does give life and meaning to the body. It comes to us pure from God. Ours is the task to keep it pure. We know that we did not fashion it. Therefore it belongs to the Creator who made it. He gives it to us and He alone takes it from us. His purpose in so doing is completely beyond our understanding. This, however, we may conclude, as does the prayer—if there is Eternal Life it is bound up with the soul, and not with the body.

"THE FIFTEEN BLESSINGS OF THE MORNING."

(A-28; B-59; S-29)

After thanking God for restoring the soul and for enabling us to awake with bodies refreshed and rejuvenated by sleep, we thank Him for restoring to us full consciousness of the blessings which He brings into our lives. These are the blessings we have no right to neglect or take for granted:

1. Ability to distinguish between light and darkness in a physical and spiritual sense.
2. Privilege of being a Jew and possessing the heritage of Judaism.
3. Freedom from bondage.
4. Manhood and womanhood—our essential humanity.

5. Vision.
6. Raiment.
7. Freedom from the bonds that imprison the soul.
8. Courage.
9. The earth.
10. And all gifts to satisfy our needs.
11. The power to walk in the right path.
12. Courage of Israel and its spiritual strength.
13. Glory of Israel.
14. Strength when we are weary.
15. Power of wakefulness and consciousness.

A SERVICE WITHIN A SERVICE

(A-29; S-30; B-67)

In ancient days religions were often intolerant of one another. "If truth is one," they contended, "and our religion is the true one, then we must combat the false one." On these grounds many attempts were made by other religions to ban the practices of Judaism. It was during one of these periods, when the religion of Israel was declared illegal, that the rabbis exhorted the people to be God-fearing in secret even if they could not proclaim their faith in public. As a matter of fact, taught the rabbis, it is more important to acknowledge God in secret and to speak the truth in our hearts. Men often worship God publicly since other people are watching their actions, but betray Him privately when no one is watching.

It was during a period of oppression that the rabbis formulated a very brief morning service consisting of the following paragraphs:

1. "A man should always revere God in private as well as in public. He should acknowledge the truth openly and speak the truth in his heart. As he arises in the morning he should say:

2. "Thou art the master of all worlds and we mortals are as nought before Thee. Before Thy power, Thy righteousness,

39

Thy wisdom, all our efforts fade into insignificance. We are weak, our knowledge is limited, often we err.

3. "What makes us significant and fills our lives with meaning is not our power, righteousness or wisdom but rather the fact that Thou didst choose us to be Thy people. Because Thou art the father, we are Thy children. Because Abraham loved Thee, Thou didst give him Thy promise at Mount Moriah that we, his descendants, would be a great people. Our worthiness stems from the altar of sacrifice upon which Isaac was prepared to offer himself to Thee. Because of Thy love for Jacob whom Thou didst call Israel we, the Children of Israel, are privileged to receive the blessings that come from Thee.

4. "Therefore we give thanks to Thee for our happiness and for our heritage by proclaiming morning and evening:

5. "Hear O Israel: the Lord our God, the Lord is One. Blessed be the name of His glorious kingdom forever and ever."

This prayer is not addressed to God. It is Israel's ancient declaration to all generations of Jews to come, to cling to the faith in One God and in the coming of His Kingdom.

6. The prayer for the sanctification and recognition of God's name in all the world.

7. The prayer for the coming of God's Kingdom of justice and peace on earth, and for the redemption of Israel.

This brief service was designed to help the people continue their appointed morning worship without exposing them too long to detection and apprehension by the oppressor. It has become part of the regular morning service so that the experience and lesson may be remembered.

SACRIFICES

At this point of the service, we read selections from the Bible and from the Talmud describing the different types of offerings which were made in the Temple. Each of the offerings represents a type of sacrifice that man must make in order to achieve a blessing. The individual offerings suggest that the

40

personal goals we cherish can be reached only if we have the will to labor and give of our strength and substance for them. It is a paradox often overlooked in an age of materialism: to receive the real blessings of life we must give up something, we must sacrifice. If people want God in their lives, they must offer their lives to His service. If people want security, they must offer justice, love, charity and a helping hand to others. Only through the offering is the blessing received. For a quiet conscience, man must give up the sins that disturb his peace of mind. If a person wants to be loved, he must first give love and friendship to those whose love he seeks.

The congregational sacrifices described in these passages dramatized the interdependence of all the members of the House of Israel as a sacred brotherhood. They taught the vital need for corporate sacrifices in order to achieve the social blessings.

In the Temple, sacrifices were offered for the peace and welfare of all nations of the world. Thus, the Jewish people taught the glorious lesson that a nation must make sacrifices for the good of all mankind if it is to enjoy the blessings of God.

The sacrificial service has been discontinued since the destruction of the Temple. The lessons of sacrifice have, nevertheless, not been lost.

THE THIRTEEN PRINCIPLES OF LOGIC

(A-34; B-83; S-32)

This is not a prayer. It is a selection for study in the middle of the worship service. This and other selections in the service are traces of the traditional service as it was once constituted. It is common knowledge that the synagogue served a three-fold purpose. The *Bet HaMidrash* (House of Study), The *Bet HaTfillah* (House of Prayer), and *Bet HaKnesset* (House of Assembly). The service in the synagogue possessed three elements—prayer, study, and charity (social action for the relief of the suffering). This was in accordance with the rabbinic conception that the world rests on three foundations; *Torah* (knowledge), *Avodah* (worship), and *Gemilut Hasadim* (acts of loving kindness). We find here a selection of study in the principles of logic because the sages felt that the laws of God can best be understood through reason and logic. Finally, every service concluded with the giving of charity. For this purpose we still have a *tzedokoh* box circulated at the end of the weekday services and in the invitation to make contributions during the reading of the Torah on *Shabbos* and Holy Days.

THE PSALM OF THE DAY

(A-35; B-91 to 99; S-34 to 39)

The practice of reciting a special psalm for each day of the week goes back to the Temple service. The psalms are very old indeed, but they have an important message for us today:

1. Psalm of the first day (Sunday), Psalm 24, asks, "Who can stand on God's holy hill?" and the answer is, "He that has clean hands and a pure heart."

2. Psalm of the second day (Monday), Psalm 48, tells us, "God is the power that makes for righteousness."

3. Psalm of the third day (Tuesday), Psalm 82, demands "Defend the poor and the fatherless, do justice to the afflicted and the destitute, rescue the poor and the needy."

4. Psalm of the fourth day (Wednesday), Psalm 94, asks those who doubt there is such a thing as moral law and that God judges, "He that planted the ear, shall He not hear? He that formed the eye, shall He not see? He that instructed nations, shall He not correct?"

5. Psalm of the fifth day (Thursday), Psalm 81, expresses God's hope, "O that my people would hearken unto me!"

6. Psalm of the sixth day (Friday), Psalm 98, declares that God's throne is eternal and immovable. The floods of heathenism, atheism, and other "isms" that deny and challenge Him, lash themselves against the rock of God's throne. They spend

themselves, but God's throne remains unmoved. The "isms" come and go, but God is eternal.

7. Psalm of the seventh day (Saturday), Psalm 92, God's righteousness triumphs over wickedness. God's faithful, the righteous, will be vindicated.

"HYMN OF GLORY."

(A-61; B-127; S-40)

This is an adoration of God. He is old and young, the evening and dawn of the universe. He is a wise old judge and a youthful fighter for justice. He is an advocate of peace and a warrior of battles. He is our King who raised us up, and crowned us with the Torah.

Truth is His essence and He listens to us when we call upon Him in truth. May our praises uttered in sincerity be acceptable unto Him. We love no one more than God. He is our Rock, our Redeemer and the only Savior we know.

The author of this beautiful poem is known to us as Judah the Pious of Regensburg, Germany (died 1217). Only a rare combination of saint, mystic, poet and philosopher, such as Judah, could have produced such an exquisite gem of poetry. The ark is opened during the *Shir Hakovod* and the verses are chanted responsively by Cantor and Congregation.

"MOURNER'S KADDISH."

(A-62; B-131; S-40)

Now the mourners conclude the first section of the morning service with a *kaddish*. Then begins the second part of the morning service, the *"p'suke d'zimra."*

The *kaddish* is an affirmation of the essential Jewish belief that life is good. Therefore men should treasure it, protect it, and use it properly. The kaddish is an affirmation of the essential Jewish belief that God's kingdom of righteousness, love, truth and peace will be established on earth. *Kaddish* is more than a prayer, it is the whole philosophy of Jewish life.

43

Preliminary Hymns and Psalms of the Morning Service
(A-63 to 79; S-43 to 59; B-133 to 168)

The second section of the morning service, *P'suke D'zimra,* consists of psalms and hymns. This second section is a logical prelude to the third section which is composed, mainly, of prayers of petition on behalf of Israel. "Let the praise of God precede any petition that we may address to Him," say the rabbis.

As we have already seen the first section of the service consists, largely, of private devotions or personal prayers. It was usual in the past, and in some communities still is, for each individual to recite the first section, personal prayers, at home or on his way to the synagogue, or in the synagogue before the public service got under way. The chanting of psalms and the singing of hymns seemed like a fitting transition from personal prayer (first section), to group or congregational worship (third section).

Most of the prayers in this second section are from the Book of Psalms; a few, from other sections of the Bible. The final prayer of this section gives us an additional reason for the insertion of a section of psalms at this point of the service.

4

Rosh Hashanah Morning Service

PART TWO

"Thou art the King enthroned on High in majesty."
(A-80; B-169; S-60)

This is the prayer of coronation in which we proclaim God our King. It is altogether logical and natural to sing the praise of God as King *before* his coronation. Herein lies the value and importance of prayer. If we want God to be our King, we must first cultivate the art of prayer, the habit of singing His praises. As we find the words and the will to praise God, He comes into our lives, other forces and powers are dissipated, and God's rule becomes established. God's Kingdom is, at least in part, established in the world through prayer.

Because *"HaMelech"* is the transitional prayer from the preliminary section to the actual morning service, the chazan takes over from the *Baal Tefilah* at this point. Beginning in a low tone, his voice rises in a gradual crescendo. The entire congregation may join in especially for the final, triumphant word *"HaMelech,"* the King. In many congregations it is customary for the *chazan* to begin chanting the *HaMelech* while standing in his place in the congregation, or while ascending the *Bimah*. Then, as he walks slowly toward the Ark with bowed head, he concludes "Enthroned on High in majesty."

THE KADDISH

(A-81; B-170; S-60)

Because we come now to the end of the second section of the service, a Kaddish is again recited. The *Kaddish* is always said at the conclusion of a section, or at the end of an entire service.

The Kaddish is in Aramaic rather than Hebrew because Aramaic was the language spoken by the Jews during and after the Babylonian captivity. The presence of this and other prayers in a language other than Hebrew is in accord with the rabbinic view that we may pray in any language that is familiar to us.

THE BORCHU

(A-81; B-171; S-61)

Borchu (Bless God) is the call to worship. It is the same invocation as is used in the evening service. "Bless Ye the Lord Who is to be blessed," was the ancient formula used in the Temple to summon the people to worship morning and evening, As the first rays of light pierced the nocturnal sky, a priest or Levite would cry out from the high tower of the temple, *"Borchu es Adonoy HaMvoroch,"* and the people, already streaming toward the courtyard, would respond with *"Boruch Adonoy HaMvoroch."*

The call to prayer is not merely an exhortation to go from one place to another, from the market place to the Synagogue. It is a call to go from one frame of mind to another: from complaint to contentment, from bitterness to praise, from despair to hope, from sorrow to consolation, and from surrender to faith.

When Moses asked Pharoah to let the people go into the desert so that they might worship God, Pharoah refused on the ground that if the people were permitted to worship God they would not return to Egypt. Pharoah was right. When men worship God, they become transformed. When men make exodus from the bondage of worldly cares to conversation with God, they move physically and mentally from bondage and weakness to freedom and strength. When men leave their Egypts to worship God, they do not turn back. Rather do they turn their eyes toward the promised land.

"Blessed art Thou Who forms light and darkness and creates peace and all things."

(A-81; B-171; S-61)

This blessing is based on a verse in Isaiah 45:7. "I am the Lord and there is none else. I form light and create darkness. I make peace and create evil." This prayer is an intellectual protest against the Persian religion, Zoroastrianism, that propounded the existence of two gods—one a god of light and goodness, the other of darkness and evil. While Judaism recognizes the reality of both light and darkness and of both good and evil, it recognizes only one God as the creator of all things.

The Zoroastrian concept of two gods is an attempt to reconcile the existence of a God of goodness with the apparent reality of evil. If a God of good desires the victory of righteousness, how explain the existence of evil and unrighteousness? The Zoroastrians solved the philosophical enigma by concluding that there are two creative and powerful forces at work in the universe. Some religions conjure up a Satan to explain the existence of evil; others solve the problem by denying the reality of evil. Evil, they contend, exists only in our minds as delusions of thought. Still others argue that all evil is of human authorship, the result of man's own doing. God creates only good; man creates evil. There are others who make a religion of Atheism (without God) and insist that neither good nor evil is real; only matter is real. Good and evil are merely our interpretations, our mental reactions to purely physical phenomena. Finally, there are some who contend that evil is a permanent and necessary aspect of life; without evil, we could not recognize good. The God who created goodness

47

created also evil; but Man, a free agent, can choose between the two. If there were no choice, he would not be free. Evil will always exist as a challenge to man's moral freedom. Evil itself thus assumes a moral function in the context of life.

Each of these theories recognizes an aspect of evil; evil has many causes and diverse effects. Judaism rejects, however, those views which deny the reality of evil completely, or which ascribe the responsibility of evil solely to men, or which interpret evil as a permanent and implacable foe of God with the stature of a god. Judaism holds the view that evil is, has a cause, and even a purpose; its existence depends upon the will of the Creator; and finally, that an ultimate decisive victory over evil will be won by man in partnership with God. We believe in this eventual victory over evil because it is possible, and desirable. We believe, also, that this victory is inevitable. There is no easy philosophical solution to the problem of evil but from the standpoint of Judaism there is only One God. As men cooperate with Him, they learn to achieve greater good and to lessen human suffering and evil.

"O King Girt with Power"

(A-81; B-173; S-61)

Here we have a *piyut* (poem), written by Eliezer Hakalir in the 8th Century, in which is depicted the ultimate victory of God, the King, over the forces of evil. It depicts the fulfillment of the prophetic vision of the Messianic Age. God fights evil; men must fight it too.

The power of God referred to in this prayer is ethical power, the power that makes for righteousness. Belief in a God who will overcome His foes and vanquish their evil is neither wish fulfillment nor naive hope, but the demand of moral man. Something in the spirit of man refuses to acquiesce to any world view which interprets the Universe and life in amoral terms, which conceives of the creative, life-giving force as ethically neutral and impotent. If righteousness (moral values) has validity, then the concept of the ultimate victory of righteousness follows logically. Our moral sense demands this victory; logic dictates it; Judaism affirms it.

"O King, Thy Word Stands Steadfast"

(A-177; B-177; S-64)

Here we have a similar *piyut* in which we reaffirm our faith in the fulfillment of God's word that the redemption will come. We appeal for the early coming of the messiah. This prayer is said on the second day of *Rosh Hashanah* in place of "O King Girt with Power." It consists of seven sections and closes with an acrostic stanza that spells out the author's name and that of his son.

The author, Simeon ben Isaac ben Abun, lived in Mayence on the Rhine in' the early part of the 19th Century. According to legend, his son Elchanan was kidnapped by gentiles and educated in the church when he was very young. The lad became a great Christian scholar and after a distinguished career in the church was eventually chosen to be the Pope. One day he discovered his true identity and effected a secret reunion with his father as follows. Knowing that his father was the chief spokesman for the Jewish community of Mayence and would head any deputation that might come to Rome to protest, he, as Pope, ordered the Archbishop of Mayence to ban Jewish observance in that city.

As he had anticipated, his father Simeon came to Rome to request audience with him. When the two were alone, the son Elchanan disclosed his identity and promised his father not only to revoke the decree but to return to Judaism. In time he kept his word, returned to Mayence, and lived as a Jew in his father's house. In gratitude for the return of his son, El-Chanan (Gracious God), Simeon composed this poem-prayer in which he enshrined the name of his son.

The poem can be appreciated without the legend but, perhaps, it has more significance when it is interpreted as an

49

expression of Jewish faith in the justice of a gracious God and as the joyful outpouring of a father whose lost son was miraculously restored to him.

"Tent-like this Day the King Stretched out the Sky"
(A-86; B-189; S-68)

Here we have another *piyut* composed by Eliezer Hakalir. Because *Rosh Hashanah* is the anniversary day of the creation (*Yom Harat Olom*), it is also the day set aside for judgment (*Yom Hadin*). Creation implies that everything has a purpose. The creatures of the universe are judged in order to determine whether or not they are living up to the purpose for which they were created. Heaven and Earth tremble because they, too, are under judgment by the Creator. From the standpoint of Judaism, even nature may not act arbitrarily. It has a purpose (the Divine intention) to fulfill, and is "morally" bound to act in accordance with the will or the purpose of God. Man, like heaven and the earth, is also God's creation and he, too, is subject to judgment. Since God created with love, with understanding, and with mercy, He judges with the same attributes. The God who created the world in love will judge it lovingly. The God who created the human heart, and, therefore, understands it best, will judge us with heart and with mercy. This, too, is an acrostic poem, its verses arranged in alphabetical order.

THE SHEMA SECTION
(A-88; B-193 to 199; S-69 to 72)

The *Shema* section is a most important part of the service. It includes two blessings that precede the *Shema* and two prayers that follow it. Let us consider briefly the prayers that constitute the *Shema* section.

1. "*Yotzer HaMoros*—Blessed art Thou, O Lord, Creator of Light."

This prayer is called the *Yotzer*, a prayer of thanksgiving to God for "combating evil, sowing righteousness, causing salvation to spring forth," and for creating besides the lights of the heavens the new light that He will cause to shine upon Zion.

2. *"Ahavah Rabbah*—Blessed art Thou who in love chose Israel for Thy Service."

A fervent prayer of thanksgiving to God for the moral and spiritual light of the Torah which foretells the restoration of Israel in Zion. Zion, Torah, and Israel will be reunited in the service of God. In this prayer we give thanks to God for the great love (*Ahavah Rabbah*) that He manifested to us when He gave us the Torah. The Jew who rejects the Torah, by design or by neglect, tends to feel rejected. The Jew who is aware of the worth of the Torah feels privileged to belong to the people which has been blessed with the greatest gift of God's love—the Torah. If we are to *experience* the satisfaction and joy of God's love, we must learn to *appreciate* the satisfaction and joy of God's love; we must learn to appreciate His Torah. If we wish to be happy as Jews, we must learn to say, "How good is our heritage."

THE SHEMA YISROEL

The opening line "Listen, O Israel, the Lord our God, the Lord is One" is the opening line of Judaism. It is the first and last principle of Jewish faith. It is to this day the first prayer taught the Jewish child and the last words of every faithful Jew. God, the Father, the Creator, the King, the Everlasting Power Who guides the destiny of nature and man, of galaxies and nations, is One.

It is in Him that all the profoundly diverse and fragmentary elements that make up life and the universe find their original oneness, and in Him alone that they can discover their ultimate oneness. Therefore, to Him alone is it our duty to pray. Through prayer we become at-one with Him.

1. *"V'ohavto*—Thou shalt love the Lord," is taken verbatim from the Torah (Deuteronomy 6:4-8).

Unlike the early religions that fostered in their adherents a fear of the gods they worshipped, Judaism taught the love of God. Just as the *Unity of God* is the foundation of *Jewish theology,* so must *Love of God* be the basis of *Jewish life.* Just as human love is indivisible and consummatory, so must our love of God consist of the service of the heart, of the soul, and of all other powers and faculties. We do not love a little or partly. Either we love completely or do not love at all.

2. *"V'hoyo*—And it shall come to pass, if ye will hearken diligently unto My commandments," is verbatim from Deuteronomy 11:13-22.

This prayer is a statement of the principle that the love of God implies the fulfillment of the moral law by men. Men should accept the moral and the ethical requirements of the Torah not for the sake of the rewards and punishments that follow from our success or failure to live up to them, but rather out of love for God. Even though we should not be motivated by the fear of Divine judgment, we are enjoined to recognize that we are subject to judgment. This judgment is not postponed until the after-life and does not take place in some remote heaven or hell. It takes place in this life, right here on this earth. We may question whether rainfall is the reward of virtue or abundant harvest results from morality, but there surely is a cause and effect relationship between man's behavior and the consequences that flow from it. A sure and inescapable punishment comes when God's laws of justice are violated.

3. *"Vayomer"* is verbatim from Numbers 15:-37-41. It speaks of the *"Tzitzis"* that are worn as a reminder of our duty to fulfill the commandments of God (the *Mitzvos*).

The three paragraphs of the *Shema* contain a rather complete program for wholesome Jewish living:

1. Dedication of heart and soul and might to God. The works of our hands and the powers of our intellect should be devoted primarily to the fulfillment of the moral and spiritual

duties prescribed in the Torah. Our worldly ambitions should not obfuscate our vision of the highest goal of Jewish life: the glorification of God. Every movement, every Jewish effort, should be motivated by this objective.

2. Maintenance of a program of Jewish education that will produce Torah-conscious and enlightened Jews.

3. Our homes and families should be built on the moral and spiritual foundation of Torah.

THE TWO PRAYERS OF THE SHEMA SECTION

1. *"Emes V'emunah*—True and firm"

The proof of God's reliability and the truth of His teachings is the redemption of the Children of Israel from Egyptian bondage. He kept His word to Israel: He redeemed us from Egypt, from Babylonia, from Rome, from the Hamans and Hitlers of all times.

2. *"Ezras Avosenu*—the help of our fathers."

Therefore, do we conclude the *Shema* section with the blessing, "Blessed art Thou O Lord, who redeemed Israel." Redemption comes to Israel through faithful devotion to Torah and *Mitzvos* (God's Law).

THE AMIDAH

(A-91 to 95; B-201 to 7; S-73 to 77)

Like The Sabbath *Amidah*, the *Amidah* here consists of seven blessings.

1. God is adored as the God who makes history and who will bring history to the realization of its ultimate purpose: The messianic redemption.
2. The second blessing adores the God who shows His creative power not only in history but in nature.
3. The third blessing adores the God of Holiness.
4. The blessing of thanksgiving for the Holy Day.
5. The blessing of thanksgiving for the old Temple service and for the return of God to the new Zion.

53

6. The blessing of thanksgiving for God's unfailing mercies.
7. The blessing of thanksgiving for peace which is the greatest blessing of all.

The *Amidah* is recited silently by the congregation as all worshippers stand facing the ark in which rests the Holy Torah, the blueprint of the blessed life. After everyone has concluded the silent *Amidah,* the ark is opened and the *chazan* proceeds with the chanting of the Reader's *Amidah.*

READER'S REPETITION OF THE MORNING AMIDAH
(A-95 to 111; B-209 to 70; S-77 to 94)

Except for the *Shema,* the *Amidah* is the most important part of the Jewish service. The word *Amidah* means *prayer to be said standing.* It is also called *Tfiloh Belachash,* silent prayer, because it is said silently by the congregation. Later it is repeated aloud by the *chazan* (reader). The *Amidah* is part of every service and contains prayers of praise, thanksgiving, confession and petition. It expresses the loftiest aspirations and the deepest concepts of Judaism.

The following comments are based on the outstanding prayers in the Reader's (chazan's) repetition of the *Amidah.*

"With the Inspired Words of the Wise"
(S-77; A-95; B-209)

The reader of the service announces that he is appealing to God in the words of the wise teachers of Judaism and of the discerning poets of Israel. The *piyutim* (hymns) which follow are prayers in poetic form which, having won the hearts of the people, were sung and recited for generations before gaining their place in the High Holiday service. Judaism believes more in the efficacy of the time-tested prayers of the group than in the spontaneous utterances of the individual. Spontaneity is desirable in prayer but time-tested prayers associated with historical events in Jewish life have greater value. The secret of Israel's vitality is its continuity with the past.

The Prayer Book and *Machzor* link the Jewish present to the sublimest aspirations of the past. A people that remembers its past will yet have a future. If we recall with reverence the inspired words of the wise men of the past, we shall be able to generate vital wisdom for generations yet unborn.

"With Humility and Apprehension," 1st day

(S-77; A-95; B-211)

This *piyut* (hymn) was composed by Yekuthiel ben Moses of Speyer in the 11th century during the time of the Crusades. He lived in one of the most trying and tragic periods of Jewish history. But nothing could destroy the faith of the poet who sang of the faith of Israel. The poet, overwhelmed by the awe and solemnity of the Day of Judgment, stands before his God with humility and apprehension. In this spirit should we face God on these Holy Days. If man had more humility, he would have more comprehension. We pray in the words of the poet, "Give me understanding." Although we are extremely advanced in scientific and technological knowledge, the world is hardly beyond the adolescent stage when judged by its moral understanding. Our technological knowledge and the power it gives us make us arrogant. Our need is for humility to make us receptive to the moral needs of our times. More than anything else the Jew prays for humility and moral understanding.

"I come to Supplicate Thee," 2nd day

(S-78; A-190; B-229)

This prayer goes back to the 9th century. It refers to God's judgment—the thought uppermost in the Jewish consciousness during the Ten Days of Repentance. Repentance is always in order. God's judgment takes place constantly but during this special period we strive, through special rites, to make ourselves deeply aware of the process of Divine Judgment. Generally, man makes excuses for his moral failures or fails to become aware of them. However, the man who fails to recognize and to repent of his moral shortcomings during these days is considered morally dead.

On New Year's Day our spiritual destiny is written down, and on the Day of Atonement it is sealed. We write it down in a penitent spirit as we greet the dawn of the New Year; we seal it on Yom Kippur with a firm resolution to avoid repeating our errors in the days that lie ahead. The New Year is approached with the hope that man will record a chapter of moral progress and spiritual achievement in the Book of Moral Life rather than a chapter of destruction, moral decadence and spiritual decline in the Book of Spiritual Death.

"Thou Art Our God"

(S-79; A-98; B-217)

Many of the liturgical poems were composed during periods of religious persecution when Israel was forbidden by church and state law to read the Torah. Jews have always met challenges to their faith, refusing to allow themselves to become a Torah-less people. When forbidden to study the Torah, they composed and sang songs containing the lessons of the Torah. In that way the words and lessons of the Torah were kept on the lips of their children to humanize the hearts of the next generation of Jews.

Were we to lack faith in our accumulated experience and time-tested wisdom in a crisis, we should perish. The secret of Jewish survival has been the ability of the Jew to cling to his faith in God and to repent his sins in time of disaster. "The beginning of wisdom is the fear of the Lord." In this *piyut* the Jew restates his faith in God, the all-powerfull Creator, the great Judge, the Reservoir of spiritual values, the Personal God who will be nigh unto him if he calls upon Him in truth.

"The Lord is King"

(S-83; A-105; B-225)

The poet, Eleazar Kalir, composed this prayer in the 7th century. It expresses the hope that some day all men will say:

"The Lord is King, the Lord was King, the Lord will be King forever and ever." A fundamental tenet of Judaism is recognition of God's Kingship. Universal acceptance of its moral implications will change the hearts and souls of all men. When men really find the road to God, they will find simultaneously the path to one another. This prayer pictures the fulfillment of the messianic vision of all mankind as one human brotherhood hastening to accept God as King.

"The King Most High"

(S-85; A-201; B-251)

This *piyut* composed by Rabbi Simeon ben Isaac of Mainz, in the 10th century, contrasts the permanent power of the divine King of the universe with the evanescent power of mortal rulers. The poet reaffirms Israel's faith in the permanent sovereignty of God. Very temporary is the power of the *"melech evyon"* the mortal tyrant who thinks he is ruler over the destiny of man. No matter how successful he may seem, a man can play the role of God only for a brief span. God's power and justice will prevail, for the earth is the Lord's.

You will recall with what reluctance Samuel appointed Saul the first King of Israel. And a King of Israel always had to vow, upon the Torah, that he would follow the law of God. Nor could he exercise absolute authority. Read in this perspective, history can strengthen us to endure the tempests of our times.

"Unto God Who Ordaineth Judgment"

(S-89; A-106; B-261)

Composed by Eleazar Kalir in the 7th century, this interesting *piyut* is in acrostic style. This device was used in Jewish liturgy to help the people memorize the prayer. Note that the first letter in the Hebrew is always "Lamed," who; that the first verse begins with *"aleph,"* first letter of the alphabet; the second, *"beth,"* second letter of the alphabet, etc., up to the last letter of the Hebrew alphabet, *"tov."* In this prayer God the Judge is described, and the virtues and characteristics associated with an exemplary judge are summarized. When most peoples still held primitive conceptions of the administration of justice, the Jewish conception of justice was well advanced:

A. *Man is given a fair trial and is innocent until proven guilty.*

"God, the Judge, searches the heart of man and uncovers evidence hidden from view, before he passes judgment."

B. *The personal convictions of the Judge are irrelevant to the decision.*

His judgment must be based on the facts in the case. "He restraineth His indignation on the Day of Judgment and uttereth knowledge in judgment."

C. *The Judge may not be arbitrary.*

"He remembereth His covenant." Even the Heavenly Judge is bound by rules of convention and by agreements.

D. *The quality of justice is tempered by the quality of mercy.*

"He showeth mercy, hath compassion upon His handiwork on the Day of Judgment, and clothes himself in charity. His robe is not the robe of authority but of mercy."

E. *The function of the Judge is to protect the innocent as well as to condemn the guilty.*

"Who sustaineth His blameless ones on the day of Judgment."

F. *The function of the Judge is to forgive and to rehabilitate, rather than to condemn.*

"He forgives the people chastened by Him in judgment, and maketh pure them that trust in Him."

In all the prayers which we read on these High Holidays we declare *Rosh Hashanah* to be a Judgment Day on which the Ruler of the Universe summons all men to account for their deeds, before His Tribunal of Justice. Most religions postpone the Day of Judgment until after death when it is too late to change a way of thinking and living. Judaism, on the other hand, sets aside certain days throughout our lifetime for periodic self-examination in order to keep the conscience sensitive to righteousness and truth. There is always room for improvement in everyone's personal life, in the Jewish community, in the American way of life, in the world in which we live. One lesson we are expected to learn during these Holy Days is— there is room for improvement everywhere and, while we live, the opportunity to make that improvement is always present. We must not accept what is. We can, if we will it, convert what is into what ought to be.

Our religion teaches us that God is the highest and ultimate Judge but it teaches us, too, that man must be his own judge, that the Day of Judgment is essentially a day of self-judgment and self-appraisal. A beautiful parable told by the rabbis teaches this.

"The angels asked the Holy One, Blessed be He, 'When is *Rosh Hashanah?*' Said He, 'Ask not me. Let us go down to earth and ask man. It is up to men to set aside a Day of Judgment'."

The function of psychiatry and of the modern art of counseling is to help people recognize their own problems and to decide for themselves what course of action is required for the most satisfactory solution. *Introspection* is the first part of the procedure; the second is *resolution*. This is precisely what our 4000-year-old religion and our age-old *Machzor* urge us to do. The purpose of the High Holidays is not to crush us with guilty feelings but rather to insure a wholesome, properly-functioning personality.

THE KEDUSHA

(S-90; A-107; B-261)

Kedusha is the Hebrew word for Holiness. The *Kedusha,* or prayer of holiness, was composed by the Spanish-Jewish poet-laureate, Jehudah Halevi, in the 12th century. This poem, or prayer, is based on three verses from the Scriptures:

1. Isaiah 6:3
2. Ezekiel 3:12
3. Psalms 146:10

The *Kedusha* consists of three introductory sentences chanted by the chazan, and of three congregational responses. The *chazan's* and the congregational portions are chanted alternately. The *Kedusha* appears always in the Reader's Repetition of the *Amidah* in the third blessing, The Blessing of Holiness. Three cardinal principles of Jewish theology are enunciated in this prayer:

1. "Holy, Holy, Holy is the Lord of Hosts, the whole world is full of His Glory."

Many people look at the panorama of life and see nothing significant. The pessimist sees chaos, the blind movement of meaningless coming out of nowhere and going nowhere, flux and commotion but no progress. Isaiah looked at the Universe and saw the glory of God.

He saw nature as cosmos, as law and order, as the manifestation of mind—Energy and Spirit, as Power moving in the dynamisms of physical reality, and the unfolding of a mysterious first cause developing toward fulfillment of a given purpose and toward a given goal. Isaiah saw WILL expressing itself in the impulse behind the upsurge of life, REASON expressing itself in the rationality of nature, POWER turning the wheels of the complex galaxies, urging the seed to become a plant, and breathing life into the inert.

Isaiah looked at man and again he saw the glory of God. In him he saw a creature struggling to find freedom, truth, goodness, and beauty. In man he saw a thinking, planning, hoping, building personality striving to realize the spark of the divine within it.

"The whole world is full of His Glory," cried the prophet. "Seeing is believing," says the skeptic. But the crux of the whole matter is *how* we see. One man sat by a singing kettle and saw nothing but a kettle; Watt saw in it a steam engine. One man dodged a falling apple and saw nothing but an apple; Newton saw the great law of gravitation. One man closed his eyes in terror at the flash of lightning and saw only lightning; Franklin saw electricity. One man, lost in the mist of the mountain, could not see the path or even the mountain on which he stood. He saw only the mist. Standing on the same mountain, Moses saw God and the moral foundation of the good life. One man looked at hieroglyphics and found them meaningless; another saw a vast culture and ancient people speaking out of the same hieroglyphics. Some look at the earth and see the promise of prosperity for all, and peace; others can see only what is in it for themselves alone. Some people look at man and see a stranger, a competitor, and enemy; others look at man and see a comrade, a neighbor, a brother.

Some people cannot see even the barest facts of life; others have just enough sight to see the facts; still others have the insight with which to see beyond the facts, and fashion new facts out of their vision. Judaism sees the glory of God in the whole world and would create and shape the facts of life in the image of that glory.

2. "Blessed is the Glory of God from His place."

The first verse, "Holy, Holy, Holy, the whole earth is full of His glory," refers to what the theologians call the Immanence of God—God is in the world. The second verse, "Blessed be the glory of God from His place," refers to the Transcendance of God—God is out of and beyond the world.

A child may be explained in terms of its psychological and physiological constitution, in terms of its appearance and behavior, and in terms of the parents that gave it life. The character, constitution, and behavior patterns of the parents are in the child. In a sense, the parents are in the child. However, the parents exist separate and apart from the child, and the child exists as a separate individual. So it is with the universe and

God. The universe emerges out of the source of all creation, God, and some of the character and quality of God are in the universe. Yet both are separate entities. God, the Creator and Spiritual Father of mankind, is in man but separate and apart from him.

A fruit or a flower may be explained in terms of its physical and chemical composition but it comes from a tree or a bush, influenced by countless factors and forces outside itself. Everything has its source in something outside self, including the whole universe, infinite as it is. The only original source, without beginning or end, is God. For want of a better term we use the word "heaven" to describe God's place from which His glory emanates, a recognition that the source of the universe and all its phenomena is outside the universe.

3. "God will rule forever; your God, O Zion, unto all generations"—

The third congregational response speaks of the timelessness of God. Everything is subject to time except God, the eternal. Just as movement can be interpreted and understood only in terms of the relation of a moving object to a stationary object, so time can be understood only in terms of something timeless. The universe and man have meaning only when viewed in relationship to God.

The quality of each of these three aspects of God has been partly absorbed by Israel. Israel lives in the world but its survival must be explained partly in terms of Divine Providence. Its spiritual constitution, the Torah, is a product of this world, and at the same time, a revelation from outside the world. Its eternal verities are indestructible, relevant to all generations. The religion of Israel has rendered the Jewish people inexplicable in exclusively biological and sociological terms.

"THE THREE THEREFORES."

(S-90; A-107; B-263)

1. "Therefore, O Lord, let Thine Awe be manifest in all Thy Works."

On *Rosh Hashanah* we pray for universal peace. War results when self-interest is placed above righteousness. When all people form one union (a real United Nations) to do God's will, the blessed era of international harmony will come. Universal acceptance of His sovereignty and His Law by all nations can usher in the Kingdom of Righteousness and the Era of Peace.

2. "Therefore, O Lord, grant glory to Thy people who serve Thee."

The redemption of mankind and the redemption of Israel are contingent on' one another. There can be no peace in the world until there is peace for the Jew. A world which mistreats the Jew is not morally prepared to create a good life. To the Jews, the brotherhood of man is not merely a pretty phrase or a polite public utterance. It is the very heart of his religion, basic to the achievement of God's kingdom on earth. So long as man fails to accept all his fellowmen in brotherhood regardless of race, color or creed, he has not accepted God in his heart. When all God's children unite in fellowship to do God's will, there will be peace and justice.

3. "Therefore the righteous shall see and be glad . . . while iniquity shall close its mouth."

When justice and peace prevail and Israel is accorded its proper place in the brotherhood of men, then will the righteous of all nations see and be glad, and the just exult.

"Hallow us by Thy Commandments . . . Blessed art Thou, O Lord, Who sanctifies Israel." (A-109; B-267; S-92)

Through obedience to God's will our lives become hallowed. *Mitzvos* train us in discipline and self-restraint. The *Mitzvos*, historic institutions and teachings of our faith, can bring joy into every Jewish home and add the quality of holiness to our lives.

"Restore the Worship to Thy Sanctuary . . . O may our eyes witness Thy return to Zion." (A-109; B-267; S-92)

This prayer refers to the service of the Temple in Jerusalem. Just as the lessons of monotheism (one God) came from the Temple on Mt. Zion in the past, so may true knowledge of God come out of Zion in the future to enlighten the world. Torah can come only from God. It is our hope that God will again use Israel as a vehicle for the enlightenment so badly needed to blot out the darkness in which men and nations grope today.

"The Lord Bless Thee and Keep Thee"

(A-110; B-269; S-93)

In the Mishnah, this benediction is called the "Benediction of the Priests." The priestly blessing was daily recited at this point in the Temple service. Since the destruction of the Temple, this blessing is recited by the reader when he repeats the Amidah.

"Grant Peace"

(A-110; B-269; S-94-

The prayer for peace is the final prayer of the *Amidah,* a congregational restatement of the Priestly Benediction in the form of a prayer. It ends with the words, "Blessed Art Thou, O Lord, Who maketh peace." Peace can come only when men accept God and follow His will. Thus ends the Reader's Repetition of the Amidah.

"Our Father Our King, we have sinned before Thee."

(A-111; B-271; S-94)

Try to picture Nazi Germany standing humbly before God and saying, "We have sinned before Thee." Try to picture any attacker of the Jew standing humbly before God and beating

64

his breast in penitence. You can't. Try to picture Soviet Russia admitting that it has made an error or that there is some inequity in its administration of justice. You can't. The Communists attribute all sin and error to the capitalists and the "enemies" of the state. The Germans say, "Deutschland ueber alles;" the Soviets say, "the working class above all;" the Jews say, "God above all." Confession requires sensitivity and humility; the attacker of the Jew is brutal and arrogant. Since we live in a world in which men must take sides, we should be glad we're on the side that says, "Our Father our King, we have sinned before Thee."

The five repetitions in this prayer of "inscribe us in a book," correspond to the Five Books of Moses (Torah):

1. The first, "inscribe us in the Book of Happy Life," corresponds to the Book of Genesis in which the *creation of life* is described. "And God saw that it was good."

2. The second, "inscribe us in the Book of Redemption and Salvation," corresponds to the Book of Exodus which tells of *redemption from Egyptian bondage*. And God said, "Let My people go."

3. The third, "inscribe us in the Book of Sustenance," corresponds to the Book of Leviticus which tells us of the *holy sacrifices and the feasts before God.*

4. The fourth, "inscribe us in the Book of Merit for a meritorious life," corresponds to the Book of Numbers which tells of the *twelve tribes descended from the Patriarchs, because of whose merit we are alive.*

5. The fifth, "inscribe us in the Book of Forgiveness and Pardon," corresponds to the Book of Deuteronomy in which Moses rebukes Israel for its sins, but gives us the technique of *Teshuvah* by means of which *we gain forgiveness and pardon.*

We pray for the blessings of Torah: *life, freedom, sustenance, righteousness* and *forgiveness*. The Torah contains the words by which Israel must live. If we wish to achieve in our lives the promised blessings, it is not enough to pray for them. We must live by them.

5

Torah Reading for Rosh Hashanah

THE PURPOSE OF THE READING OF THE TORAH
(A-114 to 130; B-277 to 324; S-97 to 123)

Because the early founders of Judaism resolved to make the Torah the possession and inheritance of the entire people, rather than the exclusive property of a small ecclesia or priestly class, they instituted the ceremony of reading the Torah in public and assigned to its study the status of religious requirement. The Torah readings, which became part of the service in the synagogue, the sermon and discussions based on the selections read, familiarized every Jew with the religious and ethical teachings of his faith. In the ancient world, this endeavor to educate a whole people in its religion was unparalleled. In religion, generally, worship is associated exclusively with prayer and its rites. In Judaism, the study of the Torah is regarded as a form of worship as well as an intellectual pursuit.

HOW THE TORAH WAS READ

In early Palestine, it took three years to complete the reading of the entire Torah. The Babylonian Jewish community, however, arranged the order of the readings so that the entire Torah could be completed in one year. Since the destruction of the Temple, we have followed the Babylonian procedure. Today, some congregations are reverting to the three-year cycle.

Originally, one person read the Torah selection, one rendered the translation so that everyone could understand and then one scholar commented on the text. When the length of the reading was increased, more than one person was called to read the sacred text aloud to the congregation. On week days, the number was 3; on Rosh Chodesh, 4; on Festivals, 5; on the Day of Atonement, 6; and on the Sabbath, 7.

At a later date, a reader (*chazan* or *baal kore*) was appointed by the congregation to read the entire text. The individual called to the Torah had to recite only the *Bracha* (Blessing). This is the practice today. The purpose behind all these changes was to keep the Torah the possession of the entire congregation even when individuals had no mechanical skills for reading the text.

THE HOLY ARK

When the children of Israel received the Ten Commandments, they built their first Holy Ark. Since the days of Sinai, the Ark, which once held the Tablets and today holds the Torah, has been an object of reverence to the Jew. However, the little house which shelters God's law is holy only when the Torah is resting in it. The Ark symbolizes the world in which we live; the world is holy (resistant to evil) when the Torah is at home in it; when Torah (Law of God) goes out of the world, our immoralities bring upon us chaos and destruction.

During the period that the Jews wandered through the desert on their way to Israel, the Ark of the Covenant was carried before them. Thus was created in them a consciousness that God, their Protector, went before them; that so long as they followed Him, they would march to victory.

THE CALL OF THE TORAH

The call to the Torah is called *Aliyah* because the worshipper has to ascend the platform from which the Scroll is read. *Aliyah* may also refer to the spiritual elevation which a man is expected to derive from the experience of ascending to the Torah. A man is called up to the Torah by his Hebrew name(s) and the Hebrew name(s) of his father, i.e., *Itschok ben* (son of) *Avraham.* The first to be called is always, if possible, a Jew of priestly descent (*Kohen*); the second, of Levite descent (*Levi*); the rest are called Israel (any Israelite). The one called to the Torah recites a blessing before the biblical portion is read, and a closing blessing immediately following the reading by the *baal kore.*

After each individual reading, it is customary for a blessing (*Mi she-berach*) to be pronounced upon the one called to the Torah. He, in turn, may exercise the privilege of having blessings recited upon others. Often, an offering to the congregation for some charitable cause or for the support of Talmud Torah (the study and propagation of the Torah) is made by the individual so privileged.

RETURN OF THE TORAH TO THE ARK

After the five who are called to the Torah on Rosh Hashanah (six on Yom Kippur) complete their blessings, a *Hagbah* (one who lifts up the Torah) and a *Gelilah* (one who rolls up the Scroll and covers it with its mantle) are called forward. The Scroll is set aside and we turn to a second scroll.

On holidays we use two scrolls (on Sabbath only one) because the portion of the Torah read for the *Maftir* (one who reads the *Haftorah*) would take too long to locate if one scroll were used. After the *Maftir* portion is concluded, a *Hagbah* and a *Gelilah* are called to ready the second scroll for its return to the Ark. The scrolls are then returned to the Ark with marked reverence and the joyous singing of "It is a Tree of Life."

TORAH READING FOR THE FIRST DAY OF ROSH HASHANAH

Contents: God remembered Sarah and gave her a son. Isaac was born on the first day of Rosh Hashanah and circumcised by Abraham on the 8th day. Sarah insisted that Abraham banish Hagar, his slave-wife, and her son Ishmael. Abraham was perplexed, but God assured him that it was for the best. The chapter concludes with Abraham making a peaceful covenant with Abimelech after their shepherds quarreled over the use of the wells at *Beer-Sheva.*

INTERPRETATION:

1. Some of the greatest blessings of life come when we least expect them, or even after we have completely abandoned hope of seeing them realized. Faith means believing that those things that should, or ought to, be will eventually come to pass. That is why the man of faith must continue to believe even when evidence is against the realization of his hopes. Sarah laughed and called her son laughter because God gave her the joy of a son in her old age.

2. God gives humanity a chance to rectify its mistakes and to realize its unfilled hopes through the children who constitute the new generation. No one generation completes the work of God. Each generation is given the opportunity to create another generation which will continue the work it begins. When God tells Abraham, "in Isaac shall thy seed be called," he is assuring Abraham that through his son will his ideals and hopes be brought nearer to fruition. The moral progress of humanity requires of parents and society that they equip children with the spiritual nurture that makes for good character and noble strivings.

3. Circumcision is the Jewish rite symbolizing acceptance of the Covenant. By this act the Jew commits his son to the fulfillment of God's Law and takes upon himself all the obligations incumbent on a Jewish father.

4. This Torah reading for Rosh Hashanah is entirely appropriate. Rosh Hashanah is the birthday of the world and the child represents our hope that the world will be reborn in better moral condition than it is in today if we properly indoctrinate our children in the Law of God.

Haftorah Reading, First Day of Rosh Hashanah

The prophetic portion is from the Book of Samuel and also deals with the birth of a child. Like Sarah, Hannah shows considerable concern for the spiritual welfare of her son Samuel. He is brought to the sanctuary and entrusted to Eli, the high priest, for instruction in the Law and in the service of God. Because his mother secures for him the proper spiritual education, Samuel becomes one of the best-loved personalities of Jewish history and a hero in the cause of God.

If, in the spirit of Sarah and Hannah, the Jewish mother of today would instruct by example in the home and lead her children to the sanctuary (synagogue and religious school), we should rear a generation which serves the cause of God, and bring about a vital rebirth in Jewish life.

Torah Reading on Second Day of Rosh Hashanah

Contents: The Torah reading is from the first book of the Bible, Genesis, Chapter 22. Abraham, the founder of our faith, is called upon to sacrifice his only son. As he is about to do so, a voice from Heaven tells him not to harm the lad but to sacrifice a ram which is caught in the bushes near the altar. Abraham is assured that because he has successfully stood the test, a good future is in store for him and his descendants.

Interpretation:

A. Just as God tested Abraham, He is always testing man. Individuals and society in every clime and age have been confronted with challenges to test the strength and sincerity of their devotion to God. Our readiness to make sacrifices for the object of our love is the test of love.

We sometimes sacrifice health, moral integrity and even family for the love of money and the sense of power which it gives us. Some, sacrifice everything for family. The patriot sacrifices for country; the humanitarian, for the sake of the human race; the artist, for the creation of beauty; the scientist and philosopher, for truth; the moralist, for righteousness and virtue. We all make sacrifices for something. The value of our sacrifice depends on what we sacrifice and the purpose for which we make that sacrifice.

B. Although all people die *of* something, the religious person is willing to die *for* something. The quality or worth of our religion may be determined by the kind of sacrifices it requires of us. Only the real atheist has nothing to live for and, therefore, nothing to die for.

C. The assurance of a good future for Abraham because he met the test is meant to teach us that something worthwhile can be achieved only if we put ourselves out, sacrifice and suffer for it. We too must be willing to make the sacrifices necessary to meet the challenge of our times. In order to have peace in the world, we may have to sacrifice some of our national sovereignty. In order to establish democracy all over the world, we may have to sacrifice our traditional condescension toward certain races in our own country and in other parts of the world. In order to ensure stability in the world, we may have to cut our standard of living so that the submerged Asiatic peoples may have the basic necessities of life. In order to have freedom and victory in the war that threatens, we may have to sacrifice some of our freedoms for necessary controls.

D. The climax of the story of the *Akedah* (binding of Isaac) teaches us that God forbids useless sacrifice, sacrifice that does not bring us nearer to Him. The literal meaning of the Hebrew word for sacrifice, *korbon,* is "that which brings us close to God."

From its very beginning Judaism recognized the barbaric futility of human sacrifice. God calls upon us to live for Him and to serve Him with righteousness. The moment Abraham discovered and taught that God abhorred human sacrifice but required spiritual surrender the heathens pointed him out and said: "He's different." When Moses warned the people not to serve God in the manner of the surrounding nations and gave them Ten Commandments by which to live according to His will, the heathens said: "That people is different." Whenever the Jews have tried to live up to their highest ideals, others have pointed to them and said: "That people is different." So long as our difference makes life more worthwhile, we should cling to it as stubbornly as did our fathers. Like Abraham, we should cherish our way of life even though it makes us "different" until such time as the world rejects some of its present practices no less abhorrent than the abomination of child sacrifice in the days of its universal acceptance.

HAFTORAH READING, SECOND DAY OF ROSH HASHANAH

The reading from the Prophets is taken from the Book of Jeremiah. The prophet hears Rachel, often referred to as the mother of Israel, weeping in her grave over the exile of her children. God bids her stay her grief and assures her that her children will repent their waywardness thereby enabling Him to welcome them back to Israel with affection. Here is a most touching example of the hopefulness with which we may be inspired by faith in God. This *Haftorah* is appropriate for Rosh Hashanah because the prophet exhorts the people to repent of the sins which separate them from God.

SOUNDING OF THE SHOFAR

When the whistle announces the noon hour or the end of the working day, we feel impelled to reset our own watch by the big clock. When the *shofar* is sounded on Rosh Hashanah, it summons us to examine our sensitive soul, to regulate it and re-set it in accordance with the perfect standard of the Torah. The soul is a delicate instrument. As a result of our lassitude and neglect during the year, it gets more or less out of order.

Maimonides offers this as the central message and challenge of the Shofar: "Awake, ye sleepers; be aroused, ye slumberers, and ponder your deeds. Remember your Creator and go back to Him in penitence. Be not of those that miss reality in their hunt after shadows, and waste their years seeking after vain things which cannot profit or deliver. Look well to your souls, and consider your acts. Forsake each of you his evil ways and thoughts, and return to God so that He may have mercy upon you."

Our rabbis, ever wont to concretize abstract ideas, tell us that the *shofar* is sounded "to confuse the Satan," who prosecutes us before God at the Throne of Judgment. Re-phrased in modern terms, the *shofar* calls upon us to subdue and check those lower impulses and traits which would condemn us before our Maker. Unless we free ourselves from the grip of bad habits, unless we uproot the weeds of selfishness, thoughtlessness, envy and greed, we are doomed to spiritual stagnation and deterioration.

> "Happy is the people that knoweth the sound of the trumpet;
> In the light of Thy countenance, O Lord, they walk."

Invested with such rich symbolism, the sounding of the *shofar* takes on vital meaning. Obey its mandate and you will conquer sin, fear and temptation. This beautiful ritual, sanctified by countless centuries of observance, can be an influence for good if its message is heeded.

In the Jewish consciousness the blowing of the *shofar* has sacred associations and is a most important part of the High Holiday ritual. The sound of the *shofar* sets in motion, in the mind of the Jew, waves of recollection of our people's past as well as solemn reflections on the meaning of life and death, of duty and destiny, of faith and Judaism. The exact meaning of the prescribed order of blasts has become obscured in the course of our long history. In order that we may recapture some of the spirit, the pathos, the excitement which our ancestors felt during the blowing of the *shofar,* let us recall some of the known reasons for, and explanations of, the *shofar* ritual:

(1) According to the Jewish tradition, Rosh Hashanah is the birthday of the world. The *shofar* tones are likened to the

sounds of jubilation, the song of joy which the universe sang when it was first created.

(2) The inauguration of a king was always accompanied by the blowing of horns. The horn is blown each year to herald the crowning of God as our King, and to announce our dedication to His rule.

(3) The *shofar* blasts are the call to repentance. They appeal to us to stop chasing shadows and vain goals which will not profit or deliver us. They remind us that, according to Judaism, there is no eternal damnation or irrevocable defeat in the realm of the spirit because repentance and regeneration are always possible.

(4) The loud sound of the *shofar* heralded the proclamation of the Ten Commandments at Sinai which marked the spiritual and moral birth of the world. Today the *shofar* reminds us of the moral regeneration of which we are capable and which the world needs so badly. The *shofar* sounds a promise of new revelations to come, for the horizons of moral progress are unlimited.

(5) The *shofar* has been referred to as the horn of the Heavenly Shepherd. Just as the shepherd blows his horn to recall the sheep which have strayed, so, through the sound of the *shofar,* does God call us back when we have strayed.

(6) In ancient Israel the *shofar* was a symbol of freedom. It was blown in the Jubilee Year when slaves were set free and men returned to their inheritance. It bids us free ourselves from the passions which enslave us and return towards the Higher Life.

(7) In ancient Israel the blast of the *shofar* at the beginning of the Jubilee Year was the signal for the poor to return to the property, inherited from their fathers, which had been sold in times of adversity. A man never lost or sold his inheritance permanently, according to Jewish law. Similarly, the *shofar* blast today bids us to come into full possession of our spiritual heritage, to return to the faith of our fathers, to take up that

rich inheritance of sublime morality and of soul-searching philosophy which we call Judaism and reclaim it.

(8) The *shofar* reminds us of *Akedah,* the readiness of Abraham to give his only son to God, and of God's last-minute command to sacrifice the ram instead of the boy. These are two distinct thoughts. First, the *shofar* should remind us that life requires of us the courage to make sacrifices for our convictions. Good intentions and sentimental sympathies are not enough. We must back up our sentiments with sacrifices. Second, it is God's wish, and also man's when he is thinking in harmony with God, that we do not sacrifice our children. Our world still fails to comply with God's wish that nations shall stop the wasteful, cruel sacrifice of their youth on the altars of war.

(9) The *shofar* blast is intended to remind us of the words of the prophet Isaiah: "And it shall come to pass in that day that a great horn shall be blown and they shall come, . . . the scattered children of Israel shall return to the land from which they were dispersed, and the land shall be restored." The hope behind this blast is being realized today by the heroism of our Israeli brethren.

(10) The blast of the *shofar* keeps alive in our hearts the hope that the messianic age will come soon; that God's Kingdom will be established on earth; and peace will reign. Thus, the *shofar* which sounds the music of creation, sounds also the music of the hope of redemption and links the beginning with "the end of days." The God who revealed Himself at Creation and at Sinai will again reveal Himself when He summons all men and nations in the final judgment by the blast of the trumpet.

6

Rosh Hashanah Musaph Service

"Here I Am—Hineni"

(A-130; B-325; S-124)

This prayer was first offered up by some obscure *chazan* of medieval Europe. The *chazan* approached his solemn task with fervor and humility and a deep sense of responsibility. Tens of thousands of *chazanim* (cantors) have used these words as their introduction to the *Musaph* service.

"Here I am, poor in good deeds, appearing with trembling awe before Him who listens to the praises of Israel. I have come to plead in behalf of Thy people who have sent me. Though I have not the moral purity to perform so sacred a task, I crave Thy grace and favor. Receive Thou my supplications as Thou wouldest those uttered by one who is fully deserving. May my congregation not suffer because of my sins and shortcomings, and may the discipline of these holy days bring us all joy, peace and spiritual truth. Blessed art Thou who listenest to our prayers."

THE AMIDAH—STANDING PRAYER

(A-131 to 42; B-347 to 47; S-125 to 36)

The familiar melody of the *Musaph-Kaddish* which we now hear brings us to the "Great Amidah." This silent prayer, the longest one of the entire year, richly deserves its reputation as the most beautiful as well. Many of its sections are recited solely on Rosh Hashanah. It contains nine benedictions instead of the usual seven.

76

The *Amidah,* often referred to as *"Tefillah,"* is included in every Jewish service. Throughout the year, the Amidah is repeated three times daily: during the *Shachris* (morning), *Mincha* (afternoon), and *Maariv* (evening) services. On Sabbaths and Holy Days a fourth *Amidah* is added in a *Musaph* service.

It is customary for every worshipper to recite the *Amidah* silently. Then the *chazan* (reader) or *sheliach tsibur* (messenger of the congregation) repeats it aloud.

Reader's Repetition of the Amidah
(A-142 to 166; B-349 to 406; S-139 to 173)

Normally, the *chazan's* repetition of the *Amidah* is almost identical with the silent Amidah recited by the worshippers individually. The only differences are: The inclusion of the *Kedushah* (prayer of sanctification or holiness) in the third paragraph, and the *"Birchas HaKohanim"* (blessing of the priests) before the last paragraph. However, on Holy Days, especially on Rosh Hashanah and Yom Kippur, there are many additions to the *sheliach tsibur's* repetition of the *Amidah.* These additions are mostly *piyutim,* related in theme to the blessings in which they are inserted.

The *piyutim* were not composed by one person or in one country. In a real sense, they are the product of the collective soul of Israel. Some of these Hebrew compositions of the eighth to the fifteenth centuries have been immortalized in our prayerbook. The rituals of our brethren in France, Italy and Yemen (Arabia) contain soul-stirring Piyutim not included in our edition of the prayerbook.

The *piyutim* are more than just poetic passages. They cloak many laws, both ritual and ethical. The expression of laws in poetic form was introduced especially during periods of persecution when the teaching of the law was prohibited.

We do not all possess the ability to compose inspiring prayers. We commune with God via outpourings of the gifted

77

souls of the past. With the revival of the Hebrew language and the establishment of a creative Jewish life in Palestine, future generations will undoubtedly further enrich the prayerbook with the fruits of their poetic genius.

THIS IS THE APPOINTED DAY (*Upad Me-az*)
(A-142; B-350; S-139)

This hymn, composed by Eliezer Kalir in the 7th or 8th century, is in the form of an acrostic. The verses are arranged alphabetically, with four words to each verse. The first verse begins with the first letter of the Hebrew alphabet and so on down to the last letter of the alphabet. In all, there are twenty-two verses.

The main thoughts as expressed by the poet are as follows:

(1) This is a day of reckoning from of old, going back to the early beginnings. Adam disobeyed God then sought forgiveness. We too err, then regret; offend, then ask forgiveness. If man erred, as he often does, and did not regret and seek conciliation, he would be unregenerate.

(2) None of us is perfect, therefore, none can escape the judgment passed on his record. Some men and nations reject God and His judgment by deluding themselves with belief in their own perfection. However, only a mental aberration makes them see themselves as completely pure with no need for self-criticism or self-improvement. In the fire of judgment our character is tempered, strengthened and purified, albeit never made perfect.

(3) On this day are tried those of high and those of low estate. God judges the people with one standard of justice. Neither riches nor poverty makes us immune to error; neither do they justify special privilege. Moses, the lawgiver, and Saul and David, Kings of Israel, prayed for forgiveness and were judged like the common man. In the eyes of God all men are equal and on this Day of Judgment they are all answerable to Him. Judaism acted always as a leveling force reminding those

of "higher" estate that before God they were not more privileged than those of "lower" estate.

"MOST HIGH" (*Tefen B'mochon*)

(A-143; B-351; S-140)

This hymn was also composed by Eliezer Kalir. It is an alphabetical acrostic but instead of beginning with the first letter of the alphabet, it begins with the last (*tov*) and runs through the alphabet backwards to the first letter (*aleph*). The main thoughts expressed are as follows:

(1) "We are assembled as warriors in the day of battle, yea, we are at war with the evil within ourselves." Too often do we place the blame for our condition on the doings of others or on forces beyond our control. The ritual and worship of the Day of Judgment are not for weaklings who evade responsibility by finding excuses for themselves. They express the courage of the man who admits that he has not lived up to the best of which he is capable, and accepts responsibility for his own failures. (It is characteristic of the moral coward to criticize and to combat evil only in others. The triumph of righteousness depends on the victory of each individual over his own evil and on his mastery of his own self.)

(2) God first ascends the Throne of Judgment in order to judge. But when we sound the trumpet thus proclaiming man's readiness to repent, He changes to the Seat of Mercy. Man must take the initial step in reaching out for God's mercy and blessings. Repentance on the part of man brings Divine Grace; selfishness and greed prevent Divine Grace from flowing freely, as intended by the merciful Father.

"HIGHEST DIVINITY"

(A-145; B-355; S-141)

In the following *piyut,* the majesty, power and eternity of God, the Divine King, *Melech Elyon,* is contrasted with the frailty, helplessness and vanity of *melech evyon,* the mortal king. Originally, each "Melech Elyon" verse was followed by a *melech evyon,* in alphabetical acrostic. However, only the first and the last of the *melech evyon* verses were retained due to a desire for brevity.

COMMENTS ON "UNESANEH TOKEF"

(A-146; B-361; S-147)

This meditation was composed, or at least reduced to its present form, by R. Meshullam Ben Kalonymos, who lived in Mayence, Germany, about the year 1000 C.E. The story which inspired this poem is recounted in a manuscript attributed to Rabbi Ephraim of Bonn, Germany, who lived during the latter part of the 12th century. It tells about Rabbi Amnon of Mayence. The rabbi was continually being urged by the Archbishop of that city to change his faith. Exasperated by the rabbi's repeated refusals, the fanatic Archbishop ordered his hands and feet amputated. It was just before Rosh Hashanah. The rabbi, dying from the effects of his wounds, was carried into the synagogue at his request. Just as the *chazan* was about to recite the *Kedusha,* Rabbi Amnon whispered, "Pause that I may sanctify the most Holy Name," and then began chanting the hymn *"Unesaneh Tokef."* He expired as he reached the final words of the prayer. Rabbi Meshullam Ben Kalonymos was said to have published this poem as a memorial to the martyr. Since then it has formed a portion of the New Year's service among Jews observing the German and Polish ritual.

A story is told about a certain Yitzchak whose family had been massacred in a pogrom. After the catastrophe, he walked about aimlessly in the debris and smoldering fires. Since life had lost all of its meaning for him, he was contemplating suicide. Amidst the ruins, he spotted a fellow Jew behind the merchant's counter of a booth empty of wares. He approached and said, "What are you doing here?" "I have wares to sell," responded the other. "I have no money," said Yitzchak. "But you do not need money," said the vendor. "I will sell this to

you for nothing if you want it." "But I see no wares," protested
Yitzchak. The Jew whispered . . . "I sell Faith—for nothing."

The keynote of our whole *"Unesanah Tokef"* prayer is
faith. Our faith in God invests life with meaning and purpose,
hope and dignity. His sufferings did not embitter the martyred
poet of this prayer. Likewise, the people of Israel, when victims
of man's brutality, did not descend to despair, did not succumb
to hatred and reprisal, nor rebel in bitterness against Providence.
With triumphant fervor and invincible trust, Israel acknowl-
edges the sovereignty of God and its own indomitable faith in
life even when its sufferings are greatest.

The enumeration of the various kinds of misfortune which
may befall us during the coming year fills us with trepidation.
Yet, we are not necessarily doomed to suffer. Our sufferings
are largely the result of our unworthiness. Do we have to persist in our unworthy acts? The evil decree which hangs over us
may be averted. By sincere regret and systematic self-control,
we can return to God (*teshuva*); by conscientious prayer
(*t'filoh*), we can bring God back into our lives; and by the
practice of deeds of justice and charity (*tsedakah*), we can
become co-workers with Him in remaking ourselves and the
world in which we live.

"BUT REPENTANCE, PRAYER AND RIGHTEOUSNESS AVERT THE
      EVIL DECREE."

The rabbis in the Midrash tell an illuminating tale concerning the creation of the world.

When God was about to create the first man, the attending
angels formed themselves into two opposing groups. Some said:
"Let man be created;" some said, "Let him not be created."
Righteousness said: "Let man be created because he is destined
to be charitable." *Truth* said: "Let him not be created for he
will be deceitful." *Justice* said: "Let him be created for he is
destined to deal justly." *Peace* said: "No, because he will always
be quarreling."

81

Through this legend the rabbis teach us that there are three outlooks on human life—three ways of looking at man. One views man as completely bad; another, as completely good. Apparently, the Almighty shared neither view. Although he foresaw the iniquities and evil of mankind, he also appreciated and foresaw the good of which man was capable. One view was completely pessimistic; the other, blindly optimistic; God's view, realistic.

The novel by Eric Knight, "This Above All," tells the story of a young Englishman who returns from the battle of Dunkirk utterly disillusioned and bitter. He feels that the leaders of his government have let their people down. In bitterness he recalls his own past, the early years of his youth, his struggle against poverty. "Why," he asks himself, "should I fight to support such a social structure?" The heroine, on the other hand, pictures the good side of English life. It is for this brighter side of things that she urges him to fight. In her final speech, after he has been killed in action, the heroine declares, "We are both right."

Eric Knight's thesis, "We are both right," is in full accord with the spirit and philosophy of Judaism and the theme of this sacred day. We do not believe with the cynic Voltaire that this is the worst of all possible worlds. Nor do we agree with the optimistic Leibnitz that this is the best of all possible worlds. Man is neither damned and all evil, nor perfect and all good.

From the point of view of Judaism, life may be compared to a garden. What grows in it, whether it is beautiful or ugly, whether it brings us happiness or not, depends on us. There are weeds in the garden of life today, weeds which destroy the beautiful flowers and trees that might bear fruit. Judaism says that the garden can be weeded through prayer; repentance and charity. If we will it strongly enough, pray for it, and work for it, we can uproot evil by goodness, ugliness by beauty, falsehood by truth. We cannot make the world perfect—the threat of weeds is ever present—but we can make it a better

82

world. However, it requires eternal vigilance to keep it free and peaceful.

"For According to Thy Name."

(A-147; S-148; B-363)

"Even until his dying day Thou waitest for him. Perchance he will repent and Thou wilt straightway receive him." In this prayer, we reiterate the conviction that God always grants us His Grace when we are ready and willing to receive it. He is like a father who desires a good education for his son who is unwilling to receive this blessing.

"Man's origin is dust and he returns to dust. He obtains his bread by the peril of his life, he is like a fragile potsherd . . . as a dream that vanishes." Man is dependent on God's Grace just as a child is dependent on the parent. God, like the parent, cannot or does not give man what he is unprepared or unwilling to receive. Only by linking ourselves with God's wishes, by making His will the laws of our lives, can we add meaning to our frail and dependent existence.

"Whose Hand Taketh Hold of Judgment."

(A-149; B-367; S-150)

This prayer, an alphabetical acrostic composed by a poet in the 7th or 9th century, is unique for its simplicity and its grandeur. Here God is pictured as the merciful Father who so loves His children that He readily forgives even the wicked ones. He is always ready to receive all His children, hopeful that even those who have rejected Him will return. Every verse in this prayer begins with, "we all believe."

THE THREE THEREFORES

(A-151; B-371; S-152)

"Therefore let Thy awe be manifest in all Thy works."
"Therefore grant glory to Thy people who serve Thee."
"Therefore the righteous shall see and be glad."
These three prayers form one unit of thought. From the

standpoint of Judaism, there is a Divine purpose in history, i.e., the ultimate establishment of a world ruled by moral law, based on recognition and acceptance of God by man. However, man must be an active agent, a co-partner under Divine guidance, in the process which we call History. These prayers are an appeal to God to hasten the establishment of the brotherhood of nations, the reestablishment of the glory and well-being of Israel, and the triumph of the moral law. Categorical recognition is given to the positive role of man in the fulfillment of these prayers.

In this prayer is voiced Israel's hope for the establishment of international peace. When all people become motivated by righteousness rather than by self-interest, and form one bond to do God's will, they will enjoy the blessings of greater harmony and peace.

In this prayer the disappearance of iniquity is considered the ultimate goal of history. That man or government which practices iniquity is the enemy of God. When the rule of arrogance and wickedness pass away and the world becomes good, the good man who frequently suffers in our world will be able to enjoy the happiness to which the righteous are entitled.

One of the most frustrating and disheartening aspects of life is that of good people suffering while the wicked seem to prosper. In a moral society, based on the principles enunciated in the first two parts of *"Uv-chen,"* the righteous will be exalted and iniquity shall close her mouth. That is what the moral law requires.

THOU HAST CHOSEN US

(A-152; B-373; S-154)

God chose the Jewish people because the Jewish people chose to accept the yoke of the Torah. The Torah presented them with a task and challenge which demanded sacrifice and self-discipline of a high order. Election conferred on them a tremendous moral responsibility.

Torah gave the Jewish people a unique role in world history. Israel became a messenger bringing the Word of God to the nations solely by the free exchange of ideas with the pagan world. The religion of the One God was to be spread by the sheer impact of its validity, not by coercion or conversion. The policy of organized Judaization was rejected from the start. Anyone may become a Jew by sincerely embracing the Jewish faith but all people are equal in the sight of God. A heathen who lives a moral life is considered more worthy of the life-to-come than a High Priest who is lax in his Jewish disciplines. Our spiritual gifts were meant to be shared unconditionally and generously.

THE THREE DOMINANT THEMES

(A-154; B-377; S-159)

The men of the Great Assembly composed three prayers to be recited during the *Musaf* (Additional Service), namely: (1) Kingship, (2) Remembrances, (3) *Shofar* Soundings. The first prayer testifies that God is King; the second, that He is Recorder and Judge; and third, that God is our Law-Giver.

The *Mishnah, Rosh Hashanah,* which was compiled in the second century of the Common Era and dates back much earlier, mentions these three prayers as part of the service for the High Holidays. The same Mishnah refers to the sounding of the *Shofar* between these prayers. Each prayer contains ten verses from the three divisions of the Bible as follows: three verses from the *Torah* (Five Books of Moses), three verses from the *Neviim* (Prophets), three from the *Ketubim* (Sacred Writings), and a final verse from the *Torah*. These verses are quoted from the Bible to support and explain the meaning of each prayer.

Each of the three prayers begins with an introductory section ascribed to the great Babylonian scholar of the Talmud, Rav (third century CE), and concludes with an appropriate blessing. These three prayers cover three basic teachings of

85

Judaism, three basic aspects of God: God in Nature, God in History and God in Revelation.

Immediately after each prayer, we read the *"Hayom harat olom."* Before we go into the meaning of the three prayers, let us examine, the *"Hayom harat olom."*

"TODAY IS THE BIRTHDAY OF THE WORLD"

Rosh Hashanah is the birthday of the world. It brings home to us the message that mankind is capable of rebirth and renewed vitality, that every individual human being can create for himself a new heart and a new life. Let us not be dismayed by catastrophe and crisis. Let us not say: "There is no hope, man is hopelessly degenerate, the world hopelessly corrupt." Perhaps in the hour of greatest darkness when all hope seems lost, when the world is torn by war and barbarism, perhaps in that very hour a new force for construction is about to emerge from the minds and hearts of some God-inspired men. "Every birth is like a revolution—Violent! Even the most gentle child enters amid screams and blood" (*Valtin, "Out of the Night."*) We must always hope that, despite the chaos of our times, a new and better world will be born.

We cannot fully grasp the meaning of the High Holidays without noting the essential difference between them and our other Jewish holidays. All our festivals are intimately related to some phase of Israel's history as a people: *Pesach,* the beginning of Israel's nationhood; *Shevuos,* the traditional day of our consecration to the Torah; and *Sukkos,* the dramatic reminder of our schooling in the desert. Rosh Hashanah and Yom Kippur, however, have no base in Jewish history. They are bound up with the hopes, aspirations and destiny of all mankind. Jews pray for their own welfare and also for the well-being of all men on these solemn days.

A faithful Jew must be concerned about the happiness of all men. Read the *Machzor* carefully. You will be inspired to learn that centuries ago when the outlook of most peoples was one of self-interest, greed and rancor, the Jewish people and its religion spoke of the "birthday of the world," and prayed, as we now pray, that "all nations may form one band to perform God's will with a perfect heart."

Judaism points out that the world is constantly being reborn in the image of man's convictions and ideas. On Rosh Hashanah we pray for the rebirth of our world in the image of God's will.

MALCHUYOS—KINGSHIP
(Begins with *Olenu* and ends with *Hayom harat olam*)

The sovereignty of God is one of the dominant themes of the High Holiday liturgy. Throughout the service we re-state our belief that God is and will be recognized by all men as King of the Universe. By declaring that God is King, we assert that there is a law which transcends the laws of Man and of the State. To this Higher Power we pledge allegiance. Men die, states collapse and fall, but the laws of life remain unchanging.

This prayer for the Kingdom of God is the Jew's confession of faith and hope that all men and nations will one day accept the rule of God which is the universal practice of justice and peace.

Some of the rabbis explain that God *is* King so we must not say God *will be* King. The Kingdom of God is immediate and real, not remote, potential and ultimate. To the extent that each of us lives in conformity with the will of God, the Kingdom of God exists within us.

ZICHRONOS—REMEMBRANCES
(Begins with *Atoh Zocher* and ends with *Hayom harat olam*)

The prayer of remembrance (*Zichronos*) is the central theme of this section. God is referred to as the Judge of men and of nations, one who remembers everything. The belief that God remembers is a key aspect of our faith.

If deeds could be completely wiped away and forgotten,

they would not count. Since God remembers even what man forgets, our deeds do count. Therefore, man is held accountable by God who judges him. Because of man's frequent failure to learn from past experience, our religion stresses the importance of remembering. "A people that remembers its past will yet live to enjoy its future." The past is that heritage of experience which helps us cope more successfully with the problems of the present and face more bravely the possibilities of the future. We must not and cannot *live* in the past but we can draw strength and guidance from the experiences and accumulated wisdom of those who came before us. If we remember the heroism of our people in the past, their determination to rise above the forces that would have destroyed them, we can be stronger in our own day. If we remember their success in living with dignity in the most tragic and trying times, we can be more resolute in our own day. If we remember their spiritual and mental accomplishments, we can enrich and make more meaningful our own lives.

SHOFROS—TRUMPET VERSES
(Begins with *Atoh Nigleta* and ends with *Hayom harat olam*)

God is pictured, in these verses, as speaking in the voice of the *shofar*. The prophets, sages and poets of Israel saw and heard God everywhere:

"The voice of the Lord is upon the waters.
The voice of the Lord breaketh the cedars.
The voice of the Lord heweth out flames of fire.
The voice of the Lord shaketh the wilderness.
The voice of the Lord stripped the forest bare."

They heard Him speaking in the voice of the winds, of rushing water, of pelting rain, in the laughter and weeping of the human heart, in the spoken and written word of man, in art, music, poetry, in the quiet song of a burning bush and in the whispered pledge between lovers.

At Sinai, He is pictured as speaking in the piercing blast of the *shofar.* Wherefore, when we recall the giving of the Law and the redemption it promises, we are required to blow the *shofar.*

According to rabbinic lore, if the blast is not strong and clear when the *shofar* is blown on Rosh Hashanah, it is because satan has entered the *shofar* and blocked the voice of God: This may sound like superstition but the heart of the legend is a profound truth. Many influences constantly block the call to moral duty and responsibility, to the summons to live up to the ethical and spiritual values of Judaism. Jews will remain an ethically and spiritually sensitive people only so long as they attune their ears to the message and summons of the *shofar,* the voice of the Torah.

In ancient times, the trumpet was used universally to call men to battle. By using the trumpet to herald the coming of peace and redemption, the rabbis of antiquity converted an instrument of bad tidings into a symbol of good news. It is not enough, tell us the rabbis, to *hear* the *shofar;* we must contemplate and understand its meaning.

THE CLOSING HYMN

(A-171; B-419; S-178)

The author of *Adon Olom* is said to be Solomon ibn Gabirol (1021-1058), the renowned Spanish-Jewish poet and philosopher whose book on religion is still used in Catholic seminaries. This supreme expression of absolute trust in God, the *Adon Olom,* is the closing hymn of most of our services. It is said before retiring at night and is often sung by those who watch the last moments of a dying person.

Certain facts of life and death cannot be explained to our complete satisfaction by reason. The afflicted ask in their pain, "Why?" When death claims the young and gifted, we ask, "Why has this happened?" Some mysteries of life must be accepted, in humility, on Faith. The religious Jew repeats the refrain of the *Adon Olom*:

"Into His hand I commend my spirit when I sleep and when I wake, and with my spirit my body also; the Lord is with me and I will not fear." Thereby, he affirms his readiness to accept God's will on faith even though he cannot understand it on the basis of reason.

7

Rosh Hashanah Afternoon Service

(A-172; B-425; S-179)

In ancient days there was a daily sacrifice accompanied by elaborate rites in the Temple of Jerusalem. This sacrifice was called the *Korban Mincha.* In the minds of the people, the *Mincha* was associated, also, with the dramatic and unforgettable contest between the prophet Elijah and the priests of Baal on Mt. Carmel. "And it came to pass, at the time of the offering of the *Mincha,* that Elijah drew near and said: 'Lord, God of Abraham, Isaac and Jacob, let it be known this day that Thou art God in Israel.' " You remember the story. The false gods and their prophets had had their hey-day in Israel. Now Elijah confounded them and showed the people who the true God was. The people, thereupon, fell on their faces and exclaimed: "The Lord, He is God; the Lord, He is God."

Mincha is probably the oldest complete service. The shortest of the daily services, it consists of the following prayers:

1. *Ashre* (Psalm 145) extols the greatness and goodness of God and describes the happiness in store for man in the true worship of God. The introductory verse, "Happy is the man who dwelleth in the house of the Lord," was added to the original psalm to teach us to spend some time in silent contemplation of our relationship with God before we begin to address our prayers to Him. Many of the prayers in our services follow

91

this pattern. They begin with a silent meditation, a general statement of philosophy or a proclamation of belief, before the address to God.

What a beautiful sentiment is suggested by the alphabetic acrostic. All the letters of the alphabet, the entire gamut of human sounds, are harmoniously united to express the glory of God. This is the message of the *Ashre*: the way to happiness is through the dedication of all man's powers to the glorification of God.

2. *Half Kaddish* divides the different sections of the service and follows each period of study within the service.

3. *Reading the Torah* (if Rosh Hashanah falls on the Sabbath) requires that only three people be called up: a *Kohen*, a *Levi*, and a *Yisroel*. It is a very brief selection from the last book of the Torah, from the closing speech of Moses to the children of Israel: "The words of God are like the gentle rain and the tender dew. God is a rock, impregnable, but giving refuge to the fearful. God is perfect in justice, faithful and merciful to His children, yet how sinful have his children been. God is like a mother eagle that protects her young, takes them up from the nest with her wings and bears them on her pinions. But, alas, they turn and soar away from her in their ingratitude."

4. *Half Kaddish* marks the end of a period of study of the Torah.

5. *Amidah* is the silent prayer.

6. The prayer *Ovinu Malkenu,* Our Father, Our King, is so called because each supplication begins with these words. This prayer for forgiveness follows logically after the reading of the Torah selection in which Moses urges the children of Israel to return to God in repentance. Our plea for forgiveness is addressed to God who is our Father and our King. Our God is the ideal father who loves his children, understands them, reproves and chastises them, teaches and guides them with compassion. Our God is merciful but He is demanding. Our

God is a King who grants us privileges but expects us to assume heavy and challenging responsibilities. We are His subjects and we should obey Him in love.

In the Talmud, the *Ovinu Malkenu* is referred to as Rabbi Akiba's Fast Day prayer. In the Siddur of Rav Amram Gaon (9th century) only 25 verses of the *Ovinu* appear. The additional supplications commemorate tragedies that occurred after the original prayer was composed. In order not to mar the joy of the Sabbath, the *Ovinu* is omitted on the Sabbath.

7. *The Complete Kaddish,* originally, marked the end of service. The central theme of the *Kaddish,* the sanctification of God, is the central message of Judaism as well. To deepen our own and our fellowman's awareness of the holiness of God so that the whole world may become holy makes life purposeful. *Kiddush Hashem,* investing life with holiness, must be our aim. Each of us can make life just a little better, holier, more godly. One of the great Jewish mystics suggests that the *Kaddish* was written in a secular language, in Aramaic, to teach us that the secular must be used to express and further the sacred. The most commonplace and ordinary act, such as partaking of food or donning new raiment, is elevated to a religious and spiritual experience by a ritual and a benediction of thanksgiving to God.

The *Kaddish* invests life with meaning, values, ideals and a worthy goal. The modern study of the human psyche reveals that man's personality breaks down when he is overconcerned about himself, when he feels and acts as though the whole world must truckle to his needs, when his self-expression is trapped within his egocentricity. The man who can attune himself to the *Kaddish* is never maladjusted because his creative expression be he poet, philosopher, businessman, politician, or just the common man reaches out of himself upward for the glory of God.

8. *Olenu,* "It is our duty to praise the Lord of all," goes back to antiquity, chronologically speaking. Ideationally, it ex-

presses an idea which is the very foundation of our religion. We have taken upon ourselves the yoke of God's kingdom and all the duties it implies. We do not say that all men must accept Judaism in order to achieve salvation. They must, however, accept God as King and let His law rule their lives. Herein is a fundamental difference between a religion that educates and religions that convert; a religion that holds up the truth for all men to see and accept, and religions that say you cannot possess the truth without formal affiliation.

Jews are often asked why they do not seek to convert others to Judaism. The answer is simple: we are not seeking dues-paying members for an organization. People do not have to give up their group identity and social affiliation in order to recognize and accept the fundamental truth of Judaism as expressed in the *Olenu*. The *Olenu* is not so much a prayer to God as a call to all men to establish proper contact with God.

It is common experience that a light will fail if the bulb does not make proper contact with the source of electrical power. Something vital in man fails too when he is not in proper contact with God, the source of life which generates physical and spiritual power. When man praises God, he is in contact with Him. When the power of God flows into man, moral and spiritual light is increased in the world. The rabbis instruct us to praise God both in prosperity and in adversity. Certainly both affect our happiness. Nevertheless, our real well-being depends, essentially, on our making proper contact with God.

Originally, the *Olenu* appeared only in the *Musaf* service of the High Holy Days, at the beginning of the *Malchuyot*, Kingship, section. Not until approximately 1300 C.E. did the *Olenu* become part of any other service. Up to that time, the *Kaddish* was the concluding prayer. Scholars suggest that the *Olenu* was added to the final *Kaddish* because it balances and completes the idea expressed in the *Kaddish*. The *Kaddish* expresses the hope that God's name will be hallowed in all the earth and the *Olenu* proclaims that all men will find harmony and brotherhood in the recognition of the One God.

9. *Mourner's Kaddish* requires us to hold up our heads in the face of death and to reaffirm the value of life. We want to believe that life is worthwhile but death fills us with fear because it shakes our faith. The fear of life can be disastrous and the fear of life enters when faith departs. The *Kaddish* is the comfort that comes to mourners from knowing in moments when we fear life that we need not be afraid of the future. In it we praise God and proclaim that a time will come when a new mankind will have less cause than we to fear life because the world will be gentler and better than it is now.

Our tradition teaches us that the proper attitude toward death is neither rebellion nor resignation. Rather are we enjoined to emphasize in our lives the highest moral values by which our dear departed lived thus advancing the Kingdom of God. This message of the *Kaddish* prayer serves as a bond between the living and the dead.

It is a real triumph when a man can banish fear of death and say, *Yisgadal*. Death should not occasion bitterness or excessive grief. Amidst our pain and our tears we should be aware and thankful to God for the gift of loved ones. Why He takes them away and, sometimes, the circumstances under which they return to Him are incomprehensible to us. Nevertheless, our faith tells us that life has a divine source and returns to it. Life is a loan from God to be returned gratefully to Him at His appointed time.

8

Yom Kippur Evening Service

THE MESSAGE OF YOM KIPPUR

The message of the symbolism of Yom Kippur is simple but meaningful repentance. A highly imaginative story by a great Hebrew writer illustrates well the importance of repentance. The author's imagination carries us to heaven.

As might well happen in heaven, as on earth, an angel was disobedient to God's command. He was summoned before the Throne of Glory, admitted his guilt, but pleaded for mercy. God looked down at him benignly and spoke thus: "I shall not punish you. However, in atonement for your sin you must perform a task for me. Go down to earth and bring back with you *the most precious thing* in the world!"

The angel thanked God for His kindness and hastened to do His bidding. He paced up and down the face of the earth rejecting one possibility after another. Finally he came upon a battlefield. There, a brave young soldier lay dying of wounds received in defense of his country and his loved ones. The angel caught up the last drop of blood shed by the dying hero and brought it before the Throne of Glory.

God looked at the angel and said: "Very precious in my sight is the courage of the fighter for noble causes who puts honor and ideals above self. But it is not the most precious thing in the world."

The angel again took up his search. At last he found himself in a hospital where a nurse lay dying from a disease contracted while nursing back to life a suffering child. The angel caught up her last breath and presented it before the Throne of Glory.

God looked at the angel and smiled: "Self-sacrifice, beautiful and selfless, in caring for the sick, is very precious in my sight. But it is not the most precious thing."

The angel resumed his tireless search on earth. One day while passing through a dark, dense forest he overtook a man on horseback, armed to kill. This man was on his way to the forester's hut determined to murder the man who had caught him poaching and had given him up to the authorities. On reaching the hut, he stole over to a little window and peered in. The forester's wife was putting the children to bed and the forester himself was kissing them lovingly as he pulled the covers over their tired little bodies. The would-be murderer remembered, at that moment, his own home and his loving family. Regret pierced him like a knife. He shuddered to think that by one pull of the trigger he might have destroyed the happiness in this home. A tear rolled down his cheek. The angel caught up that tear and brought it before the seat of the Almighty. God smiled and said: "I think you have learned your lesson now. There is nothing more precious than a tear of repentance."

Repentance is the central theme of this Holy Day: Repentance is the hope of Man and of the World.

It was customary in the synagogue of Rabbi Isserlein for the *Shamash* to ascend the pulpit each Yom Kippur Eve in order to make this public announcement: "Hearken all ye congregants. R. Isserlein begs your forgiveness for any wrong deed he may have committed. If he has ever offended or hurt you in any way whatsoever, he humbly begs your forgiveness."

It is also customary for Jews to embrace one another and to wish one another a happy New Year after the Evening Service on Yom Kippur. This is intended not so much for friends, who always wish each other every blessing, but for those who have quarrelled during the year, for friends and relatives who have offended each other. On Yom Kippur Eve, as we expect to be forgiven by God, we must first forgive one another. We must go forward into the New Year united in brotherly love in order to meet the responsibilities of our common future.

What an amazing transformation would come over our world if men and nations were to heed the moral lessons implied in these Yom Kippur customs:

1. To ask forgiveness
2. To forgive
3. To go forward in unity and brotherhood to meet our common responsibilities.

All men and all nations are *offenders* and *offended*. All must, therefore, ask forgiveness and all must forgive.

"KOL NIDRE—ALL VOWS"

(A-15; B-489; S-207)

The author and the date of the *Kol Nidre* are unknown to us. We do know, however, that this prayer was used in the service as early as the Gaonic period, in the 8th century.

The melody of the *Kol Nidre* has struck a deep responsive chord in the hearts of the Jewish people. It fulfills the counsel of Judah the Pious (13th century) who said: "Chant your supplications to God in a melody that makes the heart weep; and your praise of Him, in a melody that will make the heart sing." A noted non-Jewish poet once said about it: "Such a righteous song, redolent of people's suffering, can hardly have been composed by one brain however much inspired."

The melody of *Kol Nidre* is the song of Jewish suffering, quiet, meditative, yet free from the note of complaint or rancor. The author of the melody is unknown because, in truth, the author of the song is the heart of Israel.

The prayer consists of two parts:

(1) First comes the proclamation by the elders of the congregation that it is lawful to pray together with those who have transgressed. This has reference to those Jews who under duress (the threat of baptism or death) forsook Judaism. Down through the ages, tens, perhaps hundreds, of Jews did not have the courage to die for their faith, or to face expulsion from the lands in which they were rooted and take up a wandering existence in pursuit of freedom and peace. Many of these converted Jews came back to Judaism as soon as freedom of religion was restored or they could do so without extreme suffering. The synagogue took the position that such Jews should be welcomed back into the fold. Since many of the converts returned to Judaism on the Day of Atonement, this proclamation was most appropriate.

The "transgressors," mentioned in the prayer, refers also to Jews within the fold who had committed serious sins offending the faith. Such transgressors were regarded, by law, as worthy of complete acceptance by the congregation so long as they came in a spirit of repentance.

The recital of the *Kol Nidre* brought relief to tormented consciences. The repentant sinner could return to the God of Israel by joining His people in prayer. However, although the proclamation of the Heavenly Tribunal absolved the Jew from sins committed against God, it did not absolve the Jew from sins or offenses against a fellow Jew or a gentile neighbor.

The custom of making peace and righting wrongs with family, friends or neighbors whom we have offended, became an ethical requirement associated with the Day of Atonement. Atonement for an offense committed against a fellowman is much more difficult than atonement for a sin against God.

The story is told of a certain Rabbi Meir who delayed his arrival at the *Kol Nidre* Service, refusing to enter the synagogue until the congregants had forgiven one another for their trespasses against each other. After the congregants shouted in unison, "We forgive one another," the rabbi entered the synagogue, ascended the *bimah* (platform before the Ark) and said: "I know that you forgive one another now, but tomorrow you will resume your usual ways. You are not worthy of the service of the Day of Atonement until you promise to abide by your resolutions." "We will," they promised. Whereupon Rabbi Meir said: "Take heed. If you keep your resolutions and vows, this year will be a blessed one; if not, you know the punishment for broken promises." Then the rabbi turned toward the Holy Ark and began to chant the *Kol Nidre*. (The *Kol Nidre* cannot release anyone from a juridical oath or from any promises, contract, or obligation between man and man.)

(2) The second part of the *Kol Nidre* is a prayer for the nullification of unfulfilled promises and broken vows to *God*. Under normal conditions, and especially under precarious circumstances, men make promises to God (resolutions), and take vows which they later find themselves unable to keep. Recognizing that the broken word spoken silently with our God profanes the soul, the Jew desires to have such vows nullified on the Day of Atonement so that he may face God with a clear conscience. The formula known as the *Kol Nidre* is designed to absolve the individual only from unfulfilled vows or obligations between himself and God. In those lands where Jews, under duress, made vows to accept another faith, the recital of the *Kol Nidre* served to release the individual from the guilt-feeling and, at the same time, to retain his belief in the sacredness of the plighted word.

"Baruch Shem K'vod—*"Blessed be the Name of His Kingdom, forever and ever."*   (A-18; B-495; S-213)

The *"Shema Yisroel"* is always said aloud and conspicuously but its companion verse, *"Baruch shem k'vod,"* is said silently. This curious custom has a very interesting explanation. According to students of the liturgy, this innocent-looking verse was regarded by the Roman rulers of Palestine as a declaration of treason. Jews, by singing, "Blessed be the Name of Him whose glorious Kingdom is forever and ever," admitted that they never could accept the Kingdom of the Caesars. Correctly viewed by Rome as a slogan of revolt, it was forbidden Jews to include it in their prayers. Consequently, it was mumbled inaudibly in order to escape the keen ears of the Roman inspectors. But, once a year, on solemn Yom Kippur day, Jews would shout forth their pledge of allegiance to the Kingdom of God for everyone to hear.

Two additional reasons are to be found in traditional sources. According to the Midrash, Jacob called his sons to his bedside when he was about to die and said, "My grandfather Abraham had an unworthy son (Ishmael). My father Isaac had an unworthy son (Esau). Perhaps one of my sons is also unworthy. Whereupon all twelve sons exclaimed in one voice, "Hear, O Israel, the Lord our God, the Lord is One." Hearing this unanimous profession of faith, Jacob exclaimed, "Blessed be the name of His glorious sovereignty for ever and ever." Unlike the rest of the *Shema,* the *Boruch Shem K'vod* does not appear in the Bible and is not ordinarily said aloud. On Yom Kippur, however, the desire to assure our Father in heaven that we wish to make ourselves worthy is so great that we say the *Boruch Shem K'vod* aloud. The second reason lies in the fact that the response *Boruch Shem* is part of the song of the angels paying homage to God. Ordinarily we do not feel worthy enough to repeat it aloud; on Yom Kippur it may be recited aloud. All Israel clothed in white and spending the entire day in self-denial, worship, and contemplation is compared to angels.

This practice, like many other practices forced by persecution, became custom in Israel. To this day, *"Baruch shem k'vod,"* is said silently all year long but on Yom Kippur it is sung so that all may hear in whose kingdom we place our trust.

The Amidah   (A-22; B-503; S-218)

Before we begin the *Amidah,* a half-*kaddish* is said. The *kaddish* divides the *Kol Nidre* section from the rest of the *Maariv* (Evening Service), and prepares us for the *Amidah.* This prayer begins with the words, "Blessed art Thou," and is a direct address to God. Consequently, very pious Jews (*Chasidim*) will not speak the opening words until they attain the proper mood of reverence and fervor. First they prepare themselves mentally and emotionally to be worthy of speaking directly to God. Undoubtedly the greatest advocate of fervor and enthusiasm in worship was the Baal Shem Tov, the founder of the *Chasidic* movement.

The story is told that the Baal Shem Tov once asked a disciple to blow the *shofar* at his, the Master's, service and to prepare himself for this important task by committing to memory the complicated system of *kavanos,* special interpretations attached to each blast of the *shofar.* The student found this feat too difficult so he jotted down this information on a sheet of paper. But, alas, when he took the *shofar* in his hand, he could not find the paper. With tears in his eyes, with broken and contrite heart, he blew the *shofar* without special *kavanos.* The master approached him with a smile of approval: "You have done well. You know, in a house of many rooms many keys are needed to open all the doors. But one contrite heart will open all doors to the throne of the Almighty." In this spirit should our prayer be recited.

Preparation or knowledge is very important. We believe that an ignorant Jew cannot be a pious worshipper. Nevertheless, more important than knowledge is the attitude with which we pray. Prayer must be said with deep feeling, with reverence, and in profound sincerity.

According to the Jewish religion, there are moments when we must bow before God. Far more significant and desirable for man is to rise to address God. The purpose of the *Amidah* (standing prayer) is to raise us up, to make us feel worthy of lifting our eyes to Him. Spiritually speaking, the proper posture of man is to "stand before God," and "to walk with God."

"YA-ALEH-ASCEND" (A-31; B-521; S-227)

After the silent devotion, the reader continues with the *Ya-aleh*. The theme of the well-known poem was suggested by the twenty-four hour service of the Day of Atonement which begins with the *Kol Nidre* in the evening, is resumed early at dawn, continues throughout the entire day and culminates at dusk. The author, using the inverted alphabetical acrostic, makes a poetical and soul-stirring plea that the prayers of Israel ascend to heaven at nightfall and arrive at God's throne at dawn, so that salvation and reconciliation may come at dusk.

Religion is, to a large extent, poetry and imagination. That, however, does not make it less real. Actually, poetic fancy and the wholesome exercise of human imagination have been the driving powers behind man's search for, and discovery of, the greatest truths concerning reality. Anyone can see the obvious. Only the imaginative, with poetry in their hearts, possess that penetrating vision which is needed to see and to comprehend the subtle, hidden possibilities behind the real. The wisdom of Judaism's search for God in the heavens above, lies in the intuitive realization that the gravitational pull of nature and of life is downward. We are made of the dust of the earth, we walk the earth, we go down into the earth. Only a higher reality can we achieve through kinship with the Highest. While there are definite limitations to the heights we can achieve physically, there are practically no bounds to the heights we can reach intellectually and spiritually. The search for God is most certainly not the denial or rejection of the material world; it is definitely man's attempt to transcend the mundane, to capture the spirit of the above and to bring down to earth the moral and spiritual qualities of heaven.

The *Ya-aleh* is a beautiful illustration of the function of religion. We seek to rise at nightfall (beginning of Yom Kippur) through prayer, to the heights of the Divine, so that we may, at dusk (end of Yom Kippur), walk the earth uplifted by that which comes from God. The goal of Judaism is to teach man *"Amidah,"* to stand erect and to look heavenward.

"Selach-na—Please Forgive"

(A-36; B-531; S-231)

This *piyyut*, beginning with *selach-na*, is the work of one of the greatest scholars and Jewish leaders of the Middle Ages, R. Meir of Rothenburg. Meir was highly revered by the French and German communities for his saintliness and learning. He was by far the greatest authority in Germany in the 13th century. Once, while tarrying at Lombardy on his way to *Eretz Yisroel*, he was denounced by a converted Jew who was passing through the city with the bishop. The bishop had him seized and delivered to Germany where he was confined to a fortress. His students wished to offer the Emperor the sum of 20,000 marks in silver for the release of their leader. The rabbi himself declined to be set free lest a precedent be established whereby any ruler might extort money from Jews by seizing their rabbi. Meir remained in the fortress until his death in 1293. Even then the body was not surrendered. Many years later a great admirer of the rabbi paid a heavy ransom for the body so that he himself might in death be laid to rest by the side of his great teacher, R. Meir of Rothenburg.

The last verse of this stirring prayer is the theme of the entire prayer and merits special comment:

> "O forgive and remove the stain of disgrace from Thy children and pardon the iniquity of Thy faithful ones."

Most people have a tendency to think of themselves as virtuous and of the other fellow's conduct as disgraceful. They are, generally, more mindful of other people's faults than of their own. The Jew was always reminded to examine himself rather than to criticize others. His introspection led to the realization that no man sinneth not. Self-condemnation which induces guilt-feeling can be, psychologically and spiritually, as dangerous as self-glorification. The Jewish form of self-examination is not intended and should not lead to self-rejection or self-denunciation. It should lead, rather, to the reasonable understanding of our weaknesses and to an active desire to overcome them.

The last part of the verse, "and pardon the iniquity of Thy faithful ones," contains another very interesting thought. According to Judaism, man can and should be faithful to God; he can and should strive to be *Ish Elohim,* a man of God. But no man ever attains this state of perfection. This ambivalent concept of man as being faithful to God and yet sometimes guilty of iniquity is a realistic acknowledgment of the nature of man. Man's goal should be the highest so that he may be worthy of pardon when he does fall short of the mark. The choice is not between self-rejection and self-acceptance. The alternative recommended is constant striving for self-improvement.

"As Clay Are We"   (A-39; B-537; S-234)

This *piyyut,* the author of which is unknown, emphasizes man's dependence on his Maker and pleads for God's mercy. It pictures man as clay in the hands of the great sculptor-artist, God.

Out of context, this prayer is subject to misinterpretation. It appears to be tainted by an interpretation of life which came into Judaism via ancient Greek culture, to wit, that human life is the inescapable working-out of an external force or forces. According to the fatalism of the Greeks, man may delude himself with the belief that he is free to make his life what he will but, actually, he is trapped by a destiny which is deaf to his most heart-rending appeals. However, the prayer we are about to recite affirms that although human life is the unfolding of the will of God and we are largely dependent on Him,

He is not indifferent to our efforts. According to the Jewish conception, human life is part of the process of creation which God initiated. It is also the product of the ever-continuing creation in which man and God share. Man is not trapped but challenged and tested. The parent or teacher may test the child but the child himself determines the outcome by his voluntary exertions and ultimate choices.

"Mine house shall be called a house of prayer for all people."
(A-45; B544; S-238)

This verse uttered by the prophet Isaiah concludes the prayer chanted by the *chazan* just before the *"Shema Kolenu."* In a house of God created, nurtured, and maintained by Jews, reposes the spiritual possession of all mankind; everyone is welcome to it! When we pray in the house of God today, we pray for the redemption and enlightenment of all children of God. Historically, the temple and the synagogue served as a model for the church and the mosque. The particular language, architecture, or name of the house, i.e., synagogue, church or mosque, was not of telling importance. Historically, Judaism rejoiced in the fact that hundreds of millions of people accepted the fatherhood of God in their own way. It insisted, however, on its right to remain steadfast in its loyalty to pure monotheism and refused to be converted by threat or force to either of the faiths which had emerged from it. It dedicates itself, generation after generation, to the perpetuation of ideas which must eventually bring us and all mankind to the brotherhood of man under the fatherhood of God. Then will His house be truly the house of prayer for all the people.

"Shema Kolenu—Heavenly Father, Hear Our Cry"
(A-45; B-545; S-238)

While the mood on these Holy Days is sometimes melancholic, sometimes meditative, and sometimes joyous, the mood of this prayer is definitely one of deep pathos, of travail and of tears. Our forebears wept profusely as the words of this prayer penetrated their hearts. The translation in the prayer book is correct but lacks the imagery, the music, the associations, and the full force of the original Hebrew. In this prayer is contained the most fervent personal thoughts and hopes of the Jew as he stands before God.

Our parents and grandparents wept especially over the verse, "Do not cast us off in our old age; when our strength is ended, do not abandon us." From the standpoint of Judaism children are the gift of God, and parents, as His representatives, have a very definite duty to teach children the Torah, to bring them into marriage and to equip them morally and spiritually by cultivating in them an appreciation for good deeds (*Torah, chupah* and *maasim tovim*). Because of the nature of their function, parents become very wrapped up in the lives of their children. Literally, they live for their children. When the children are grown and the parental function has been fulfilled, parents often cling tenaciously to old memories and try unsuccessfully to maintain their hold on their children. They should, rather, rejoice in the independence of their children and find new interests and resources with which to fill the emptiness of their lives. Here is the fervent prayer of Jewish parents— that when children abandon them so they may build their own lives, God will be with them in their old age and grant them the resources with which to live usefully.

God moves in mysterious ways His miracles to perform. When parents successfully meet their duties toward their children, their children never abandon them. Parents who give their children *Torah* knowledge and understanding, not only build up their children but build the foundation for a relationship of common interest that will continue to keep them intellectually together. Parents who really prepare their children for *chupah*, Jewish family life, equip their children with the ritual that blesses the Jewish home and provides a common denominator of interest and enjoyment which continues to function as a meet-

107

ing ground for parents in old age and their grown children. The unique ritual, prayer, song, and ceremonial associated with family reunions on the Sabbath and festivals, and on special religious occasions, both joyous and sad, strengthen the family bond and prevent a complete spiritual rift between parents and children. A permanent bond is forged when parents habituate their children in *maasim tovim* and inculcate them with interest in communal needs and social service. A mother and daughter engaged in Hadassah relief work have a common and enduring interest in communal needs and social service. Father and son active in philanthropy and synagogual affairs have common ground on which they will continue to meet even when social interests and especially the age differential may create a normal gulf between them.

"Ki Anu Amecho—For we are Thy people and Thou, our God"
(A-45; B-545; A-238)

This prayer, rather than "As Clay are We," expresses the Jewish conception of the relationship between God and man.

We are Thy children and Thou, our Father;
We are Thy flock and Thou, our Shepherd;
We are Thy vineyard and Thou, our Keeper;
We are Thy subjects and Thou, our King.

"Oshamnu—We have trespassed"

(A-46; B-547; S-239)

The Berditshever Rebbi once delivered the following very brief but powerful sermon: "A world turned topsy-turvy, I see before my eyes! In years gone by, Jews spoke the truth in the streets and in the market places but in the House of prayer they told a lie. Now it is the other way, on the streets and in the market places they speak falsehood but in the House of prayer they tell the truth. A riddle? Here then, is the explanation: Honesty and good faith were the torches lighting the path of the Jew in the olden days. And so they made good the scriptural word of a righteous Aye and Nay, and all of their trading was done in good faith. But when they came into the House of Prayer, they would beat their breasts and say: 'We have trespassed, we have defrauded, we have robbed." That was a lie for they had been true to God and to their fellow-men. Today, in their trading they lie and defraud and, in the confessional prayer, they speak the truth."

"Al Chet—For the sin which we have sinned"
                                      (A-49; B-551; S-241)

These two prayers, *"Oshamnu"* and *"Al Chet,"* constitute the Jewish confession. You will observe that each of these confessional prayers is followed by prayers in which we seek forgiveness. Atonement is more than a wish for forgiveness; it is the desire to be *at-one* with God. To be *at-one* with God implies a desire to "bend our will to God, to observe His precepts and to revere His Law in truth." Confession starts us in the direction of sincere conversion to God and results in atonement only when we identify ourselves with God and His Law so that we become *at-one,* so to speak, with Him. Confession in Judaism is intended to give the Jew a feeling of relief. More than that, it is to alert him to his shortcomings and to strengthen his will to achieve the higher moral stature of which he is capable.

Confessions in Judaism, you will notice, are always in the plural: *"We* have sinned, *we* have transgressed," etc. They are always meant to be said by the entire congregation, even by those individuals who feel that *they* themselves have not been guilty of the sins enumerated. The reasons for the use of the plural and the recitations of the confessions by the entire congregation are manifold.

When one Jew sins, it is as though all Jews have sinned. This is in accordance with the principle that all Jews are responsible for one another. The confessional prayers for the High Holidays are constructed to intensify our feelings of responsibility for one another, for our fellow co-religionists, to make the most of life. Every important occasion in the life of the individual Jew is the subject of a public ceremony or rite in which the whole congregation participates. When an individual Jew celebrates, the whole community rejoices; when he weeps, the community shares his grief with him; when he sins, the whole community shares his sin. We share in the sin in the sense that the standard of the whole community is affected by the sin of any individual or individuals who are part of it; we share in the sin in the sense that some member or all of the community may be either directly or indirectly responsible for the individual's failure; we share the sin in the sense that we are condemned, criticized, or held accountable by God as a group for the conduct of each individual member of it. We read the entire confessional,and in the plural, to emphasize our togetherness and the mutual responsibility even in adversity and sin.

The group recitation of the confessional is intended to remind us that our ancestors knew long ago what the world is just beginning to recognize, namely, that the failure of the individual is very often the result of the shortcomings of the society or community in which he lives. The individual's sin is often a symptom of broad social diseases and the immoral texture of the larger community. A society which spends more on war and on the implements of mass destruction than it does on education and social welfare, is responsible to some extent for the destructive sins committed by individuals.

According to Judaism, the individual and the group make their confessions directly to God. There are no priests in the synagogue. The whole house of Israel is looked upon as a kingdom of priests and each Jew can turn directly to God without the assistance of an intermediary. The function of the rabbi is to *teach,* not to act as the middleman beween Jew and God.

You will notice that the "Oshamnu" is alphabetically arranged and that the sins enumerated in the "Al Chet," also, follow the alphabet. For each letter in the alphabet, a sin is enumerated. This was probably arranged as a mnemonic device, an aid to memory, before printing was invented.

"Anenu—Answer us, O Lord, answer us"

(A-53; B-561; S-245)

Does God answer our prayers?

From the standpoint of Judaism, God the Creator is concerned with the well-being of every one of His creatures. He, therfore, listens to and answers our prayers. He does not always answer us to our satisfaction. He does not always do what we would like Him to do and, of course, he does not answer us in the same manner in which we would expect an answer from another human being.

Before we examine the evidence for the belief that God answers our prayers, it is necessary to answer another question.

What Kind of Prayers are Unworthy of an Answer?

1. Requests that are contrary to His moral Law.
2. Requests that are contrary to His natural Law.
3. Insincere prayers.
4. Those which are bad for us or hurtful to anyone else.
5. Prayers intended as a substitute for action or as an evasion of our personal responsibility.

Evidence for the Belief that God does Answer our Prayers.

1. Often, in a state of fear, man prays for help and emerges with new confidence.
2. Often, in a state of weakness, man prays for help and emerges with new strength.
3. Often, man begins prayer depressed and troubled in spirit and, at the end, finds uplift and peace of mind.
4. Often, man begins prayer in a state of confusion and ends with new *insight,* an essential kind of vision of which the eyes and mind alone are not capable.
5. Often, man begins his prayer with a question and emerges with *the answer.*

6. Prayer quickens our awareness, heightens our resolves, and strengthens our will power.

7. Prayer generates in praying man the courage to do what seems impossible to rational man.

8. Prayer keeps the mind and the will of man on desirable goals and worthy values.

9. Prayer helps us feel nearer to God and neutralizes the terrible feeling of loneliness that often pervades man.

10. Prayer relaxes man, and aids his recovery from illness; often, it spells the difference between life and death, especially when the will to live is heavily involved.

Does prayer bring results? Yes, indeed! *If our prayers are worthy they help us physically, psychiatrically, morally, and spiritually.* The fact that prayer does help indicates that something in the nature of life and in the picture of man and the universe responds and reacts to our prayers. This response is the foundation for our faith that God answers our prayers.

"Mi-she-ana—He who answered"

(A-54; B-563; S-246)

Our faith in God is not based on blind belief or wishful thinking. It is the crystallization of Israel's optimism based on history.

(1) *"He who answered Abraham on Mt. Moriah when he faced the greatest trial of his life, will answer us too."* There, God diverted the sword from Isaac and promised Abraham that a great nation would come forth from his seed. In that very mountain which would have been the Mount of Death, the scene of the end of the Jewish people, He had the Temple built.

On that same mountain today, stands the great University of Jerusalem, a symbol of the indomitable will of the Jewish people to live in order to think and to contribute intellectually and spiritually to the growth of the world.

(2) *"He Who answered Jacob at Beth-El will answer us."* Remember Jacob fleeing from the wrath of his brother Esau.

He was alone, afraid, and everything seemed to be completely lost to him. Then he had a dream. In it he saw a ladder, reaching from the earth into the sky, and angels climbing up and down the ladder. He then realized that he was not alone, that God was with him. Therefore, he called the place Beth-El, House of God. His fear was allayed by the realization that the forces of Divine protection are ever with man. They sometimes seem to ascend and depart from us, but they are also descending and ever with us. He who gave Jacob at Beth-El the vision with which to conquer his fear and to face the future, will equip us with the vision and the wisdom that comes from Beth-El or House of God everywhere in these troubled times.

(3) *"He Who answered Joseph in the pit will answer us."* When his brothers had thrown him into the dungeon to die, Joseph called upon God. He was rescued, redeemed by a caravan of merchants going to Egypt, and lived to become a prince of Egypt and the rescuer of his people. When the Nazis threw the Jews into the concentration camps to die, little did they realize the impetus they were giving the descendents of Joseph to rise from the dungeons of death, to fight for the reestablishment of the state of Israel, and to live again on free Jewish soil.

(4) *"He Who answered Moses at Horeb"*—After escaping from Egypt to avoid the wrath of Pharoah, Moses fled to Midian where he became a shepherd for the house of Jethro, the Midianite. That the suffering of his people would be alleviated or that they could again become free seemed impossible to Moses. He committed the error so many of us make when our faith is weak: he pictured cruel power as invincible, and the weak as inevitably and eternally oppressed. He lost sight of the redemptive power of God, our guarantee that oppressors eventually collapse, that power destroys itself, and that the enslaved must be freed. One day, while tending the flock in the desert near Horeb, he saw a miraculously burning bush. The lowly bush burned but was not destroyed. Moses quickly realized

113

the symbolism: the burning bush was Israel; the burning bush was the oppressed, the molested, the tortured, the burned that cannot be destroyed. The burning bush was God. His enemies may try to destroy His will in the world, but He cannot be consumed, for He is eternal. Just as God inspired Moses with faith and the courage to face Pharoah and to demand freedom for his people, so will He give us vision and the courage to fight for freedom everywhere for everyone.

(5) *"He who answered our fathers at the Red Sea"*—As our ancestors stood at the Red Sea and saw the pursuing foe behind them, they became panic-stricken. Some said: "Let us throw ourselves into the sea and drown (suicide)." Some said: "Let us wait and see what will happen (senseless procrastination)." Others said:"Let us pray to the Almighty God." And the people prayed. Whereupon God answered Moses and said, "Why do you pray to me? This is a time for action—Go forward!" The people went forward—the waters divided—and they reached the road which led to the Promised Land. He who answered our fathers will also answer us when we are in the midst of a crisis. He will inspire us to go forward, intellectually and spiritually, toward a better world for mankind just as our brethren are streaming toward the Promised Land. We can, if we will it, open up new Red Seas that block the way to greater freedom.

(6) *"He Who answered Phineas when he arose from amidst the congregation"*—Many Israelites accepted the invitation of the women of Moab and Midian to a sacrificial festival, joined them in the worship of their idol, Baal Peor, a worship that involved the most licentious sexual rites. When Zimri boldly brought a woman into the camp of Israel and flaunted his immorality in the sight of Moses and Israel, he was struck down by Phineas, the young son of Aaron, the High Priest, who thus destroyed the evil that was infecting Jewish character. This act of Phineas won atonement for the people before God. He who gave Phineas the strength to stay the moral plague which

threatened Israel then, will give us the strength to stay the moral plague which threatens to engulf our world today.

(7) *"He Who answered Aaron with the censers"*—The followers of Korach rebelled against Moses and Aaron and sought to win the people over by their clever demogogy. When Korah challenged the authority of Aaron and declared that all people were priests, he was not arguing for the sake of Heaven or for a democratic cause. Korah's attempt to depose Aaron was simply a device to win authority and power for himself. Aaron was the people's leader in religion and was conducting the priesthood honestly and conscientiously.

Moses told Korah and his followers, and Aaron, to fill censers with incense and to burn them before the Lord in order to determine whose sacrifice was acceptable before God. The Bible tells us that the Lord accepted the burning incense of Aaron and consumed Korah and his followers thus vindicating Aaron. He who came to Aaron's help then, will vindicate the righteous and destroy the demagogues who speak falsehood in order to gain personal power in our day.

(8) *"He Who answered Joshua in Gilgal"*—When the children of Israel and the priests bearing the Holy Ark came to the Jordan, they were able to pass through because the waters of the Jordan were cut off. Joshua was thus magnified in the eyes of the people just as Moses had been at the Red Sea. Joshua, a new leader, did not yet have the complete confidence of the people and himself did not feel competent to take the place of Moses. Because he was worthy, God came to his help and strengthened him in the eyes of the people. Just as God gave competent leaders in times of crisis in the past, so will He give our generation the leadership it needs to meet the problems of our day.

(9) *"He Who answered Samuel in Mizpah"* The children of Israel, having been conquered and subjugated by the Philistines, yearned to return to God. Samuel said, "If you are truly repentant and wish to return to the Land, put away the foreign

gods; serve God in truth and he will deliver you from the Philistines." The people gathered together at Mizpah, drew water, and poured it out before the Lord (a form of worship), fasted on that day, and cried unto the Lord, "We have sinned against our God." Then Samuel prayed to God for the people that He might forgive them for the sins which had weakened them, thereby making it possible for the Philistines to subjugate them. Meanwhile, the Philistines, hearing of the gathering of the people at Mizpah, came up to do battle with them. As the enemy drew nearer, Samuel prayed for the people. The Lord roared, the people fought, and the Philistines were routed.

There is a lesson for all of us if we wish to defeat the Philistines of our day.

(10) *"He Who answered Elijah on Mount Carmel"* You will recall the dramatic episode described in the Book of Kings. Elijah challenges King Ahab who led the people in the practice of idolatry and taught them to follow false prophets. On the mountain, the prophets of Baal prepare their altar and lay out their bullocks as a sacrifice to Baal. Elijah does the same but dedicates it to God. The prophets of Baal call on their god from morning until noon saying, "O Baal, answer us," but to no avail. When midday was past, Elijah mocked them before the people, called upon the Lord, and said, "Hear me, O Lord, that this people may know that Thou art God!" Whereupon the fire of the Lord fell and consumed the offering of Elijah. Then the people knew that they had been following the false prophets of the false gods and the lies of a misleading ruler. There are false prophets in our world today, and men still worship false gods. Those of us who are the spiritual descendents of Elijah, the fighting prophet, have faith that the Lord will show Himself, in His way, and that the prophets of falsehood who sap the moral fibre of our world today will be rejected. He who answered Elijah will answer us by keeping alive the spirit of struggle against idolatries of our day.

(11) *"He Who answered Jonah when he cried in sore*

distress in the bowels of the whale"—Man cannot run away from responsibility. There is God's work to be done in the world and we must do it. He who taught Jonah the meaning of responsibility to his fellow man will teach us our responsibities toward others and their duties toward us.

(12) *"He Who answered Hezekiah in his sickness"*—The prophet Isaiah had prophesied that Hezekiah would die. However, God reversed His own prophet and added fifteen years to the life of King Hezekiah. A tear saved Hezekiah. The tear of the repentant and the righteous will elicit the help of God and annul an evil decree. He who saved Hannaniah, Mishael and Azariah in the midst of the fiery furnace; Daniel in the Lion's Den; Mordecai and Esther in Shushan, where Haman would have destroyed all the Jews in Persia, and He who answered Ezra when he sought to rebuild the Temple and to strengthen the Jewish people in Judaism, will answer us. Our people have gone through the fiery furnaces and have not been destroyed. Our young Israeli Daniels have fought the Arab lions and have not been conquered. Our Ezra's are laboring today to repair the damage done to Judaism by the tempests of modern "enlightenment," by the blows delivered to it in the mad rush for emancipation.

Our history teaches us and inspires us with this faith: We believe that He shall answer us by helping us to discover the answer to the perplexing problem of our times.

"Ovinu Malkenu—Our Father, Our King"

(A-55; B-565; S-247)

It is not in a spirit of self-righteousness that Israel offers these supplications before the Throne of Mercy. The Midrash, moral writings of the ancient rabbis during talmudic times, tells us that "as soon as a man has the moral strength to see himself as he is, and makes the confession: 'I have sinned,' the powers of evil lose their hold on him."

The powers of evil are ever ready to take possession of

117

every man's or every people's soul. We can resist these powers only by determined and consistent rejection of their persuasive influence. We can purge ourselves of them once they have entered us (and there is no man or people that has not at one time or another succumbed to them) by expressing repentant awareness of them and by recognizing that no force requires that they hold sway over us.

9

Yom Kippur Morning Service

The preliminary sections of the Yom Kippur morning service are the same as those of Rosh Hashanah. The first section is the "Blessings of the Dawn." The second, or transitional section, is called "Verses of Song." The third section may be referred to as the "Coronation."

We begin the morning service with prayers of thanksgiving for the blessings of life. We continue with prayers of praise to God from whom these blessings come. We then join in proclaiming God our King and in pledging our highest loyalty to him. The *"Hamelech"* prayer introduces the Coronation section.

"Hamelech—The King"

(A-33; S-255; B-581)

There are prayers which stress the importance of works and good deeds, of virtuous and righteous conduct, as the proper expression for service to God. We also have prayers, like *"Hamelech,"* in which are stressed the importance of the service of the lips. "By the *lips* of the upright art Thou exalted, by the *words* of the righteous art Thou blessed, by the *tongue* of the faithful art Thou sanctified." Worship is also a means of serving God.

The *"Hamelech"* and other prayers like it do not negate or deny the importance of "doing." They simply emphasize that good ideas and well-chosen words can influence our destiny and the quality of the world, and thus serve as instruments

119

with which we can serve God. It is good to express our thoughts and feelings verbally as well as in action through *mitzvos*. Because we accept God as King with our lips, our conduct must be governed by rules of righteousness. Saying should lead to doing. To say, "I believe," is beautiful, but the validity of our faith is confirmed by our acts. It is easier to tell what a man really believes from what he does rather than from what he says but we need both the *words* and the *works* of faith.

In science we picture an atom as a small ball. In religion we picture God as King. The atom is not a ball and God is not a King. Just as the scientist finds the image of the ball useful, our fathers rejoiced in the kingship image and found it meaningful. The ball persists in the imagery of the scientist and the King persists in the poetry of our religion. His royal crown, His scepter, His seraphic retinue and court, are significant symbols in the language of religion. Those who reject religion on the ground that it is often fancy and poetry, pathetically mistaken for substantial truth, should reject the scientific conception of the atom on the same ground. An atom is a field of energy which is very real but which we still can neither see nor completely understand. Similarly, a king-sized representation of a very real, albeit invisible and only partially understood God is a product of man's limited version but exalted aspiration to know God. To truly picture Him we cannot, and yet picture Him we must. The mental image of God as King is a useful and necessary symbolism. We must think of Him in terms of personal relationship so we can commune with Him, be inspired by Him, depend on Him, be responsible to Him, love Him so deeply that we can love *nothing else* too much, and fear Him so reverently that we can fear *nothing else* too much.

PRAYERS FOR LIGHT

(A-34 to 38; B-583 to 93; S-256 to 60)

Several prayers and *piyutim* petitioning God for light are inserted here in the blessing called *"Yotser Or,* Creator of

Light." This entire section is, therefore, known as the "*Yotz-ros.*" The familiar hymn "*El Adon,*" which is part of the *Yotzros* section, is a joyous song of praise to God, the Creator of the celestial light-giving bodies. The *Yotzros* section begins with the *Yotzer* blessing—"Blessed art Thou . . . who gives light to the eyes of those who wait for pardon . . . who forms the light and darkness . . . and creates all things." It ends with, "*L'El asher shavas,*" the bright luminaries which Thou hast made ever render unto Thee Glory.

Light is a highly revered element in Judaism. The Torah is referred to as the Eternal Light and as a lamp to light the way of man; Israel is exhorted to be a light unto the nations; Isaiah calls upon the House of Jacob to walk in the light of God; and the psalmist speaks of God as "my light and my salvation." In Holy Scripture light signifies the inner illumination that derives from an understanding heart and mind. The association of God, Torah and Israel with light denotes that the function of religion is to further understanding. The light of God, the potential of understanding with which He has endowed man, helps us penetrate the darkness of ignorance and falsehood and emerge with the discovery of goodness, knowledge and truth.

In Scripture, light also means joy, happiness or comfort. Like physical light which brightens the atmosphere and cheers us, spiritual light (light of God) heightens the morale and renders us joyful. The joy of the Sabbath and festivals, for example, glows when the lights are kindled. The solace and comfort of God's light bring serenity to and strengthen the hearts of those plunged in grief.

In Scripture, light also means freedom. We are restrained in darkness since we fear to tread as we grope about. In light we enjoy freedom of movement in the physical and in the intellectual, moral and spiritual realms of life.

In religion, God's light is symbolic of truth, beauty, freedom,

121

goodness and joy. And the quest for God's light leads man to holiness.

When Adam saw the first sun descend and darkness cover the earth, he fell to his knees in terror and prayed to God for forgiveness and light. In the beginning, man associated light with normalcy, goodness and peace; and darkness, with crisis, evil and danger. Man starts life with a mortal fear of darkness which he outgrows as he matures. Some of the ancient peoples so feared darkness they evolved a conception of gods based on that fear. They pictured the world as ruled by two forces, two gods—the god of light (goodness) and the god of darkness (evil). Judaism, on the contrary, maintained that God is the Creator of all things, of light and of darkness, of good and of evil, of life and of death, of comfort and of pain. Judaism insists that man has the moral freedom to choose between these alternatives but enjoins us to make those choices which lead to increased light, to greater goodness and to more abundant life.

In Judaism we should not fear darkness, pain, insecurity or death. Fear leads to anxiety, anxiety causes phobia and, before we know it, the complex becomes a compelling force toward the kind of conduct which is antithetical to what Judaism expects of us. Rather than fear, we are enjoined to understand, transcend, combat or, sometimes, just accept. All phenomena are part of God's creation and God's purpose. If our approach is one of faith, intelligence and courage rather than fear, we may begin to perceive their meaning in the natural order of things.

PRAYERS OF HOLINESS
(A-39 to 41; S-260 to 262; B-593 to 597)

The prayers for light are followed by prayers proclaiming the holiness of God. When we live by the light of God, we achieve in our lives the quality of holiness. This section opens with the vision of the prophet Isaiah in which he portrays the angels and all the heavenly host worshipping God and proclaiming His holiness. The Hebrew word for angels (*malachim*) means, also, messengers. The forces of nature are the messengers (angels) of God because they carry out His purpose. In carrying out God's purpose they hallow Him proclaiming, "Holy, Holy, Holy—*Kodosh, Kodosh, Kodosh.*"

KODOSH (HOLY)

(A-39; S-260; B-595)

This 10th century piyut is written in the alphabetical acrostic form. The poet describes the various ways in which God's holiness penetrates the experience of man.

The setting for the poem is heaven. Angels, awed by the holiness of God, chant "Holy, Holy, Holy," before the Throne of Glory. When we chant this prayer in the service, the synagogue becomes heaven and the worshippers become the *malachim,* the messengers and the servants of God. When men everywhere come under the influence of God's holiness, the earth will become a veritable paradise. Only one word separates heaven from earth—*kodosh.*

Many are the ways of holiness; varied are its paths.

There is holiness in a lab when a vaccine is discovered
to destroy diseases.

There is holiness when nations meet to beat swords into
plowshares.

There is holiness when we strive for purity and harmony
in family life.

There is holiness when men of different backgrounds work
together for a common future.

There is holiness when men seek justice and struggle for
righteousness.

There is holiness when men create lasting poetry or song
or philosophy.

There is holiness when men gather to seek Thee, O God,
through prayer.

"Holy, Holy, Holy, is the Lord of hosts."

THE SHEMA SECTION

(A-41; S-263; B-599)

Obedience to God, as to man, is sometimes motivated by fear and sometimes by love. The rabbis preferred the motivation springing from love. "He who serves God in *love* stands higher than he who worships because of *fear*." Motivation is important but action, the actual serving, is paramount. Love that does not end in service is not really love and is less adequate than a fear which *does* move us to serve.

"The beginning of wisdom is the fear of the Lord," but it is only the beginning. The story of religion is summed up in the efforts to convert fear into love by inculcating faith. Faith transforms fear into love. To fear is human; to love is divine.

With scientific objectivity many have talked themselves out of both their humanity and divinity in relationship to God. Multitudes believe in God in an inconsequential sort of way. They "believe" in God with the same emotion as one believes in the validity of a chemical formula, a mathematical rule or a principle of physics. They regard God as a tenable philosophical theory or an intellectually necessary hypothesis. Or, perhaps, they are conventionalists who stick to belief in God because it is the proper thing to do. There are many ways in which an inconsequential, cooperative and platitudinous belief in God exists in many minds and gives the impression of wide-spread religion. But that is not religion. Religion has not arrived until faith in God leads to positive action, until men fear Him and, especially, love Him with all their souls and substance.

"EZRAS AVOSENU—HELP OF OUR FATHERS"

(A-43; B-603; S-265)

This is a prayer of joyful thanksgiving for the Divine Providence which rescued Israel from its attackers in the past. It is, at the same time, a prayer of petition for the establishment of the Divine Kingdom in the future. The prayer is followed by the battle-cry of the Maccabees, "Who is like unto Thee, O

Lord," and reaches a climax with the proclamation, "God will rule forever and ever." It ends with the blessing, "Blessed art Thou, Redeemer of Israel." As we conclude this prayer, we rise for the morning *Amidah*.

REPETITION OF THE AMIDAH

(A-53; S-265; B-623)

It is sometimes said that the *Machzor* contains too much repetition; that repetition lengthens the service without adding new ideas and tends to dull, rather than inspire. The critics would perform major surgery on the *Machzor,* cutting out as much of the repetitious material as possible. While there is considerable merit to the argument that undue repetition should be avoided, it is desirable to understand the reasons for the repetition so characteristic of our Services.

In the first place, repetition is basic to the learning process. We learn by repeating lessons over and over again. After we read the *Amidah* individually and silently, the *chazan* repeats it aloud. This appeal both to the auditory and visual senses strengthens the prayers in the memory of the worshippers. The framers of the prayerbook used this educational technique to fix the prayers in the minds and hearts of the people. The repetition was, furthermore, intended for those who could not read or could read only very poorly. They were advised to repeat the words with the *chazan.* Many of our people learned fluency in reading of the holy language by this means. Short cuts are helpful in the learning process but patience is even more rewarding.

Although the repetition of the *Amidah* by the *chazan* has the same structure and contains most of the fundamental prayers of the worshippers' *Amidah, piyutim* and prayers are added which amplify and interpret the basic prayers and, thus, serve as a sort of commentary on the *Amidah.*

Finally, there is this to remember: The Jewish people has always striven to conserve for every Jew all the best products

125

of our religious literature. Every Jew had a right to know the poetry of the people's soul as expressed in the hymns, songs and prayers composed through the ages. Consequently, many unique literary products which expressed the Jews' quest for the spiritual found their way into those places in the liturgy where they fitted in with the theme of the service. Much beautiful and spiritual poetry survived by insertion in the prayerbook.

Piyutim (*liturgical poems*) in the Amidah

The Hebrew word is derived from a Greek term meaning poems. Some *piyutim* in our *Machzor,* and many other *piyutim,* were written over a thousand years ago and come from almost every land where a creative Jewish community existed. One group of *piyutim* is called *"selichot."* The Hebrew word, "selichot," means forgiveness and the *selichot piyutim* are prayers of appeal for divine forgiveness.

Sometimes the *piyutim* tell a story of persecution and complain against oppression:

1) "We are abused, spat upon, treated like mice in the street."
2) "We are trampled upon, threshed like straw and crushed as in a winepress."

More often, the *piyutim* uplifted the people in their sorrow and gave them the perspective from which to view fanatic oppressors and barbarous baptizers. Baruch Spinoza, the philosopher, once wrote: "The heaviest burden that men can lay upon us Jews is not by persecuting us with their hatred and scorn, but by planting hatred and scorn in our souls." The singers of the synagogue who wrote *piyutim* were more interested in the soul of Israel than in the nefarious deeds of their self-righteous persecutors. Out of their suffering they taught strength:

1) "Because I fear the one Lord God, I fear amongst the many—none."
2) "Endure dispraise for serving Him Whose name is One."
3) "Never be through idols raised to power and might."

Despite all the misery of the Middle Ages, the *piyutim* never ceased to be religious. The tone of some of the songs is fierce and condemnatory but never hateful and never cowardly. The poets of the synagogue never used their power of song to spur the people to blind hatred, to secret plotting, to vengeance or to working harm in retaliation. Instead, they sought to maintain a feeling of self-pride, to cultivate hope and to "lift up" the eyes of the people to the hills "whence cometh help."

"Aymecho—With trepidation in my heart I offer my prayer."
(A-53; S-274; B-623)

The first *piyut* in the morning's *Amidah* was written by Meshulam Ben Kalonymus of Rome in the 10th century. It is the prayer of the *"Shliach Tsibur,"* (messenger of the congregation), declaring before God his unworthiness and inadequacy to represent the congregation. He appeals to God to accept his prayer on behalf of the people, nevertheless.

"Ad Yom Moso—Until the day of man's death dost Thou wait for him to repent." (A-56; B-629; S-275)

This prayer is an alphabetical acrostic also composed by Rabbi Meshulam of Rome. It is a brief, simple, but complete philosophy of life:

Concept of God: He is the sole Judge who renders judgment upon men and nations alike. No secrets can be kept from Him and no mysteries are beyond His comprehension. His purpose and His standards of judgment are sometimes beyond man's ability to understand.

Concept of Man: Man is impure and imperfect, very definitely not the center of the universe. He must remember "whence He came, the pit that will mark his grave, and unto Whom he must render account." If he forgets these things, he may sin against his Creator.

Concept of Life: Man is born to trouble and toil. His life is beset with difficulties and conflicts, with clamor and weariness, with pain and tragedy.

With faith in God, however, he can still lead a good, satisfying life. If he labors for truth and justice during his life, acquires a good name, lives a useful life, and brings blessing into the lives of others, his "day of death is better than the day of birth." If he repents his errors, lives by his strengths and virtues rather than by his weaknesses and vices, he will be worthy of immortal life.

This is the view of the poet. It expresses only one of the moods of Judaism but it is not an authentic and complete picture of the Jewish conception of life.

"Ato—Thou art Our God"

This is another alphabetical acrostic ascribed to the poet Eleazar Kalir, an 8th century *paitan*. In verses beginning with each of the letters of the alphabet in order, the poet describes God in the following terms:

1) Abiding in heaven and earth
2) Acclaimed by multitudes because of His power
3) Speaking and creating
4) Eternal
5) Seeing even that which is secret to man
6) Wearing a crown of salvation, garbed in a garment of righteousness, dressed with a robe of zeal, and girt with justice.
7) Counselling man, working truth, and answering those who call upon Him in sincerity.

PIYUTIM ABOUT THE GREATNESS OF GOD
(A-58 to 77; B-633 to 663; S-277 to 286)

Several alphabetical acrostics by the poets, Meshulam the son of Kalonymos of Rome, 10th century, and Eliezer Hakalir of the 8th century, follow in succession. All of them speak of the greatness of God. The first *piyut,* "*Moreh* (A-58; S-277; B-635)—Thou who showest sinners the path in which to walk," is based on Psalm 145 and calls upon all men to live for the glory of God. Only one letter (*nun*) is missing both in the Psalm and in the poem based on it. The Talmud tells us that the *nun* was omitted because it is the letter with which *nofeles* (fallen) begins. It is interesting to note that the Septuagint (Greek translation written by the Jews) inserts a verse beginning with the word *neeman* which means faithful. Faith prevents us from falling from the path of virtue.

The second poem (A-64; S-280; B-645) is called "*Emor*— Say ye unto God." and calls upon us to recognize how God manifests Himself to man. A third piyut is called, "*Maase Elohenu*—How good is the work of our God." "Ascribe ye strength unto God; There is none like unto Thee; Thus will we glorify Thee; Thus with awe will we acknowledge Thee our God, and Therefore Exalt our God," are all piyutim in the alphabetical acrostic form. The poets try valiantly to describe God but, despite the poets' efforts, we must agree with the philosopher who said that God begins where human speech leaves off. It should be noted that some *Machzorim* contain more *piyutim* and some less.

"And thus, all shall acclaim sovereignty unto God."
(A-77; B-661; S-286)

The final poem before the *Kedushah* is the "*El orech din,*" composed in alphabetical acrostic. All the poems speaking of the greatness of God are intended as preparation for the *Kedushah.* We are called upon, in this section, to concentrate upon the divinity so that we may be able to come into His presence as we join together in the *Kedushah*. After the *Kedushah*, the cantor continues with the repetition of the rest of the *Amidah*. This repetition is followed by the Torah Reading for the morning of the day of Atonement.

10

Torah Reading for Yom Kippur

MORNING SERVICE

(A-110; B-711; S-309)

The section from the Torah (Leviticus 16) describes the ritual connected with the Day of Atonement as it was observed in the earliest days of Jewish history. We read of the sacrifices (a young bull for a sin-offering and a ram for a burnt-offering) which our ancestors brought before God. We also learn of the incense sacrifice and the ceremony of the scapegoat which dramatizes the casting away of sins. Finally, we are told of the fasting of the people, abstinence from work and the rites of the *Kohanim*. These rituals were observed through the centuries until the destruction of the holy temple in Jerusalem. With the change in conditions in Jewish life, brought about by the destruction of the Temple and the exile of the Jewish people from the land, the religious life of the Jewish people did not collapse. On the contrary, it matured, adjusted, and blossomed forth into higher forms of the spirit.

From its inception the Jewish people were particularly sensitive in awareness of God. This religious consciousness expressed itself in the sanctification of conduct and in cultivation of ritual. Tragedy could not shake or destroy the will of the people to find ways and means of expressing their identification with God. The ritual of Israel changed according to the exigencies of the times, but the religious rites always served to keep the people in tune with the divine. We read of these ancient rites by which our people sought to atone for their sins and draw closer to God in order to remind ourselves of the need for purifying ourselves of the sins which separate us from God and of the importance of removing the evils which estrange us from our neighbors.

It has been said that ritual begins where words end. Ritual is the language of religion. It is a means to express emotions, attitudes and ideas for which words are inadequate. It is the unspoken poetry of the synagogue and part of the language through which we converse with God. It is the discipline of the religionist. It helps us tame our baser desires and impulses, and to develop the best that is in us. It is no accident that during periods of wild dissipation in the history of the world the Jew practiced sobriety. It is no accident that during the medieval plagues which struck others hard, the Jew kept his body clean because his ritual required a curb to his carnal desires. It is no accident that Jewish family life was always strong and pure. Our ritual bound the family together and taught each member self-control and the need for purity.

Our ritual is, in part, the reenactment of Jewish historical experience. Through our ritual we perpetuate the experiences and faith of our ancestors and draw into our being the wisdom and courage of their lives. Ritual is the common bond that ties us to Jews of every age and every land today, as always.

As our unique ritual drops out of the life of our people, our connection with God breaks down, poetry dies on our lips, faith perishes in our hearts, our discipline weakens, our purity deteriorates, our strength falters, our memory lapses and the bonds of brotherhood which unite us are torn to shreds.

HAFTORAH READING

(A-114; B-719; S-315)

No one hated hypocrisy in religion more than the prophet Isaiah and the rabbis of Israel who selected this chapter

132

(Isaiah 57:14-58:14), for reading on the Day of Atonement. The prophet Isaiah chastises those who adhere to the form of fasting but violate the spirit of Yom Kippur. If rite does not lead to right, then it is wrong; if ceremony does not lead to higher morality, then it is inanity.

If we fast because it is good for the stomach, or merely because it is the traditionally accepted way of observing Yom Kippur or, if we fail to fast, considering it a hardship imposed upon us by the severe discipline of an ancient religion, we miss completely the spiritual experience which fasting can and should be.

If fasting on this holy day does not strengthen our self-discipline, our moral fibre and our determination to live a better moral and spiritual life, then it is a wasted gesture. If fasting does not help to arouse in us understanding and sympathy for the poor and oppressed, the submerged and the downtrodden everywhere, then it has failed to have its effect on us. If fasting does not help us to remember the martyrdom of our ancestors and the suffering of our brethren, if it does not quicken our sensibilities and our devotion to the needs of our fellowmen and to Jewish life, then it has failed in its purpose.

The purpose of fasting on this holy day is not to inflict torture on ourselves. The purpose is to express contrition, to demonstrate self-discipline, to give the body as well as the mind a chance to participate in repentance, to give us a taste of hunger so compassion for the needy will be alive in our hearts, to enhance our appreciation of the great but common blessings we tend to take for granted, to detach us from normal pre-occupation with the material so we can give ourselves over fully to consideration of the great spiritual needs of life. The meaning of fasting on Yom Kippur is beautifully illustrated by Rabbi Israel Salanter's "canceling of the fast." During his lifetime cholera struck the city of Vilna where he was rabbi. Many people died of the plague. On the afternoon prior to Yom Kippur, the rabbi announced that fasting on Yom Kippur would

133

be prohibited, that the service would be shortened, and that people were to take long walks in the sun. The people, however, could not believe that the rabbi actually meant for them to violate the sacred ritual of the holiest of days. In order to convince them, he ascended the *bimah* and, standing before the Holy Ark, had his *Shamash* bring him some food, made the proper blessing, and ate it in the presence of the whole congregation. As he looked into the eyes of the startled congregants, he slowly said, "It is not that we think less of *Yom Kippur*. It is that we think more of the importance of life." This story captures the essential meaning of the message of today's *Haftorah*. We must capture the spirit of the law. Conformity to the letter of the law is not enough. The purpose of the law in Judaism is to heighten our appreciation and enjoyment of life. Therefore is it written in the Torah about the use of the laws, "and thou shalt live by them."

YIZKOR, *the Memorial Service*

We pray for our dead. Why? Do the dead live? Is there a life of the soul after the death of the body? "Why not?" asks one of the sages. The rabbis reasoned that if God could make a living being out of something inert, inorganic, a clod of earth, matter that never had life, then surely he can take something that once had life and make it live again.

Our sages instruct us to remember three things: whence we come, where we are going, and before whom we stand. There is only one certainty. The destiny of the embryo in the womb, of the person in this life and of the soul in the next life is in the hands of the Creator of life. If we can appreciate the miracle of a living being emerging from the junction of two microscopic cells, then it should not be too difficult to envision a higher life for the soul as it leaves this world. The embryonic life in the womb has no idea of its hereafter anymore than it is given to us to know what awaits us in the next life.

Do the dead need our prayers? We call upon God to remember (*Yizkor*) the sainted souls of our loved ones. God does not require our prayers to remind Him. Whether they need our prayers is far less important than the awareness that we need to pray for them. Whether we remember and how we remember makes a profound difference in our lives. We should remember thankfully the good things our parents did for us, their sacrifices made to nurture and build us. Otherwise we would be ungrateful. We should remember the joys we brought them, the care and affection we brought to them. Otherwise we would feel unworthy. We should remember with kindly understanding the times they offended us, failed to comprehend our needs and wants, humiliated us. Otherwise we would be unloving and lacking in mental and spiritual growth. We should remember the times when we failed them, resented and hurt them and neglected them. Otherwise we ourselves could not understand and make allowances for our children.

One of the recurring and predominating themes of the High Holy Day services is the concept of *Z'chus Avos;* the prayers and virtues of the dead are considered when God judges us. The Bible tells us that Moses interceded on the behalf of the children of Israel when God was about to destroy them for worshipping the golden calf. According to the *Midrash,* Moses asked for the children of Israel the same opportunity God had offered when Abraham pleaded on behalf of Sodom and Gomorrah. God agreed to spare the entire people if ten virtuous men could be found. Moses could count only seven. Whereupon he turned to God and queried, "Do the dead live?" God's answer in the affirmative emboldened Moses to plead, "Then remember Abraham and Isaac and Jacob, thy servants." The Lord replied, "*Salachti,* I have forgiven." If the dead live, they can influence our destiny; if they can influence our destiny, they live.

The Jewish people has the vigor to survive because its ancestors strove so mightily in its behalf in the past. Our own virtues did not produce the Bible, the Talmud, and the rest of a great literature of Israel. Our virtues did not initiate the wonderful freedom and security of American life today. Our Jewish heritage was amassed by the merits of our fathers. Our American heritage was secured by the founding fathers of our country, our pioneering predecessors, the known and unknown soldiers of history and life everywhere who sacrificed that they might pass on to us a worthy heritage. Let our memories keep them vigorously alive. They can give us the strength and inspiration to ennoble our own lives by deeds of worth. What greater tribute can we pay to the dead and what greater good can come to us?

Our beginning is in the generations that were but our unending spirit is in the generations yet to be. Our spiritual and intellectual inheritance and our physical heritage have knitted us to the past. We are the present and also extend into the future. Our personal life determines to some extent what and how much is passed on to the unknown generations of the future.

Characteristic of the Jewish spirit of unity with the past is the beautiful custom to recite the *"El Mole Rachamim"* for Israels' sainted dead at the *Yizkor* service. The whole congregation joins to honor the great Jewish leaders of the past, the loyal and brave common people of every generation who lived their Judaism devotedly and died bravely, when necessary, *"Al Kiddush Hashem,"* in order to sanctify God's name and to bequeath to us something of real worth.

On *Yom Kippur,* as it is customary to pray for the souls of the dead, charity is given and pledged in their memory. In the *Talmud, Horayos,* 6a, *Keritos* 26a, it is stated: "It is written (Deut. 21:8): 'Forgive, O Lord, Thy people of Israel whom Thou hast redeemed.' This atonement brings forgiveness for the generation that departed from Egypt because the verse reads 'whom Thou has redeemed,' and that generation was already dead." In *Sefer Hasidim* it is stated: "Because of this Talmudic explanation, it was ordained that prayers be offered and charity given for the sake of the dead" According to the *Midrashic* commentary *Sifre,* "Forgive Thy people" refers to the living and "That Thou hast redeemed" applies to the dead. From this the rabbis concluded that the dead need an atonement and that the living must help to redeem them.

The custom of praying for the souls of the dead on *Yom Kippur* is an ancient one. It was not until the late medieval period, however, that the *Yizkor* was added to the services on the last day of Pesach, Shevuos and Sukkos.

11

Yom Kippur Musaph Service

REPETITION OF THE MUSAPH AMIDAH

On Yom Kippur we have five *Amidahs*. One *Amidah* is recited during the *Maariv* (evening service), one in the *Shachris* (morning service), one during *Mincha* (afternoon service), and, finally, the fifth *Amidah* of the *Neilah* (closing service). As we have noted before, the general structure is always the same. All *Amidahs* contain three introductory blessings of praise and three concluding blessings of thanksgiving. Only the middle section varies according to the theme of the occasion.

THE FIRST BENEDICTION
(A-134 to 135; B-763; S-349)

In this first blessing, called *Avos*, we praise the God of the patriarchs Abraham, Isaac and Jacob. The faith that sustained them nourishes us too. They were born in an age which had no knowledge of God, and they discovered Him. We, who have inherited the spiritual experience and moral virtues of our founding fathers, should surely be able to rise to greater spiritual and moral heights. We see each generation starting with the accumulated moral and spiritual wealth bequeathed to it by its righteous ancestors. The pace of man's spiritual growth is necessarily slow. Each generation makes its mistakes.

There are painful retrogressions in the moral life but we give thanks to God Who so constituted man that he can inherit and benefit from the experience of his predecessors.

We have faith in man, that wonderful creature who has discovered God, reached out for ideals, learned to pray, cultivated conscience, and struggled toward self-mastery, toward love of fellow man and obedience to the divine. We do not deny that the *Yetzer Horo,* the evil inclination in man, seems overwhelming at times. However we do not put our trust in today's prophets of despair who distrust progress and scorn to believe in the goodness of man.

We have faith in the God Who showed himself to Abraham, to Isaac and to Jacob and helped, saved and protected them. We have faith in God who appeared to our ancestors as the Emancipator from bondage. No matter how discouraging the conditions of our times, how profound the anxiety with which men regard the future, we shall continue to believe in Him as the Redeemer Who will save us even if we are unworthy. He will save us because of the merits of our patriarchs and because of His own lovingkindness if not for our own sakes. We have faith in the God Who is the master of all things and bestows blessings and lovingkindness upon His children.

During the opening words we perform a ritual which symbolizes the power of faith to transform and uplift man when he is downcast. At the word *boruch,* we bend the knee; at *atoh,* we bow; at *Adonoy,* we stand erect. Our religion requires that we worship God in joy. How can one worship God joyfully when bent under a burden of sadness and bowed down with suffering? The answer of our religion is: let him say *Boruch Atoh,* and as he comes nearer to *Adonoy,* he will be raised up. Our faith in the nearness of God (Adonoy) uplifts, gives us reason and strength to carry our heads high, and renders our hearts happy as we contemplate our future and our destiny.

THE SECOND BENEDICTION

(A-135 to 137; B-767 to 769; S-349 to 350)

This blessing is called *Gevuros,* powers of God. We praise God as omnipotent in nature, as the Provider of man, as the Protector and Redeemer. We praise God for the miracles performed daily in the natural order, in history, and in the life of man. Before the end of the second blessing which concludes with the words, "Blessed art Thou, O Lord, Who revives the dead to life eternal," we read a *piyut,* probably written by Eleazar Kalir of the 7th century: "*Enosh aych yitsdak*—How can man prove himself innocent before God?"

The *piyut* is related to the general theme of this blessing. The poet concludes that man's virtue can be established only by the mercy of God in Whose hands man is like the potter's clay. Interesting, and characteristically Jewish, is the suggestion of the poet that man can do something to prove his innocence and to achieve eternal life even though his forgiveness depends on God's mercy. He can, and should, confess his sins and repent. He can, and should, accept the Torah as a guide during his earthly pilgrimage. He can, and should, avoid the concentration of his energies on the pursuit of material goals which will bring him recognition in the eyes of his fellow man: "Gold and rich treasures will not help him or ransom his soul in the hour of death." He can, and should, follow the laws of kindness and justice. These enduring values will march before him as he goes to meet the glorious Creator in Whose hands is the power to grant eternal life to man.

THE THIRD BENEDICTION

(A-138 to 155; B-771 to 803; S-350 to 364)

This blessing is called *K'dushas Ha-Shem* (sanctification of God's name). Praises are sung to the holiness of God. How empty is the life of a man who does not feel, at one time or another, the sense of reverence that grips us when we are in the presence of the sacred. The Jew daily draws from his consciousness of God a feeling of exultation that makes it possible for him to say, "Holy! Holy! Holy!" with *kavona*.

Before the end of the third blessing which concludes with the words, "Blessed art Thou, O Lord, the holy King," we read a series of *piyutim* which are related to the theme of the benediction. Included is the *piyut "Al tizkor lanu"* (Remember not unto us our iniquities) by Eleazar Kalir (7th century), the *piyutim "Imru Lelohim"* (Say unto God) and *"Maase Elohim"* (Great is the work of our God) by Meshulam ben Kalonimus of Rome (10th century), the *"Unesane Tokef"* (We will observe the holiness), the *"Kedusha"* (Prayer of holiness), the *"V-chol Maaminim"* (We all believe) by the poet Yanai (7th century), and, finally, "V'yeh-ehsoyu kol" (All the world shall come to serve Thee.)

Unesane Tokef

(A-149; B-789; S-357)

The hymns leading up to the *Unesane Tokef* have as their central theme God's holiness as manifested in His merciful deliverance and redemptive forgiveness. The *Unesane Tokef* itself is probably the best known of the High Holy Day prayer poems. It pictures God judging mankind one by one as a shepherd counts his sheep. God reviews the deeds and determines the destiny of every soul—who shall live and who shall die, who shall be bowed down and who shall be raised up. On Rosh Hashanah He writes down the decree and on Yom Kippur He seals it. The hymn concludes with the statement that repentance, prayer and charity have the power to change man's fate and to avert an evil decree.

There is a tendency today to discard the notion that man determines his own destiny, that responsibility and accountability for his conduct is the burden of the free moral agent. In modern thought, circumstances, conditions beyond our control, limit our free determination and, consequently, our responsibility for our conduct. We are the pitiful and helpless products of conditioning. If we are such automatons, then in effect we have no souls, so how and why should we be subjected to divine judgment? Does man determine his own fate or does he just have the illusion of freedom?

The Greeks had an answer—Prometheus bound. Hellenist fatalism held that man is bound by forces beyond his control.

Christianity has an answer—divine determinism. Man is bound by original sin but can find redemption through faith in the "Son of God." Man cannot change his fate even through good works and, perhaps, not even through the saving faith. Only the unearned "grace of God," God's will, can save man, thereby determining man's fate.

Marx had an answer—economic determinism. Man cannot change himself. Economic forces, alone, determine man's fate.

Modern humanism has an answer—self-determinism. Man's will is the decisive factor in determining his fate.

Judaism also has an answer—embodied in the *Unesane Tokef*—the human will *in the service of God* can change the fate of the world. Through prayer we can change our relationship with God, through repentance we can change ourselves, and through the practice of righteousness and charity we can change our relationship with our fellowman. By dedicating our will to the service of God seriously and sincerely, we can change the course of our lives and the fate of the world. This is the way of the holy life and this is the central lesson of this Holy Day.

THE MIDDLE SECTION, THE FOURTH BLESSING

(A-155 to 191; B-803 to 863; S-364 to 399)

The middle section of the *Amidah* consists of several prayers related to the general theme of the fourth blessing which concludes with the words: "Blessed art Thou, O Lord, Who sanctified Israel and the Day of Atonement." We shall consider the most important of these prayers, beginning with the *Olenu*.

OLENU (A-157; B-807; S-366)

The *Olenu* is said to have been composed by Joshua as the Children of Israel entered the promised land. He wished to impress upon them the idea of their distinction and of their dependence on the One God precisely in that moment when they were about to enter into personal contact with the pagan peoples and religions of Palestine. Scholars of Jewish liturgy attribute authorship of the *Olenu* to the talmudic rabbi, Rav, who is believed to have composed other *piyutim* in the *Musaf* Service of Rosh Hashanah. The *Olenu* first appeared, and was used exclusively, in the *Musaf* service of the High Holy Days until the 14th century. Then it was made the concluding prayer of the daily liturgy.

The popularity of the *Olenu* that led to its incorporation into all services is readily understandable. Many of the great saints of the Middle Ages died heroically by the sword and by fire with this song on their lips. The dying prayer of martyrs became, appropriately, the final prayer of the living congregation. Also, this prayer, which expresses so beautifully the hope for the ultimate union of humanity in the recognition of one God, seemed a fitting final note on which every service should conclude. The *Olenu* expresses the same sentiment as the *Kaddish*—the messianic hope of Israel and the spiritual goal of humanity. However, since the *Kaddish* is not a congregational prayer and it seemed proper to conclude the service with a prayer in which the whole congregation joined, the *Olenu* served that purpose admirably.

The normal posture of the Jew in conversation with God is the informal and relaxed sitting position as with a Friend and Father. When we address the King of the universe, the *Amidah* (standing) position predominates. During the *Olenu,* we bend the knee, bow and prostrate ourselves when we some to the words *korim U-mishtachavim u-modim* to show our complete submission to our Master. In most congregations only the cantor bows and falls before the Ark of the Lord.

143

THE AVODAH
(A-159 to 178; B-811 to 837; S-368 to 380)

The *Avodah,* service of the High Priest in the Temple on the Day of Atonement, is another part of the fourth blessing of the *Musaf* service. Here is the exciting and magnificent ritual associated with the entrance of the High Priest into the Holy of Holies on the most sacred day of the entire year. Awe-inspiring preparations preceded those precious moments when the High Priest met God in the chamber of mystery and destiny to pray for the people and to receive the verdict. The hearts of the people stood still and lips moved in silent fervor during these moments of great decision. When the priest finally emerged, he was greeted with a great ovation followed by ecstatic jubilation.

The *Avodah* is based on records preserved in Leviticus, Chapter 16, and in the *Mishnah Yoma.* Briefly, the ceremonies and observances described in the *Mishnah* may be outlined as follows:

1. Seven days before the Day of Atonement, the High Priest was taken from his house to the Counselor's Chamber of the Temple.

2. Throughout this seven day period he participated in the offerings, burned the incense and trimmed the lamps.

3. The Elders of the Court came to instruct him. They read before him the prescribed rite for the day and said: "My lord High Priest, do thou recite with thine own mouth lest thou has forgotten or lest thou has never learned.

4. The High Priest was permitted to partake of food and drink but, on the eve of the Day of Atonement toward nightfall, he was allowed to eat only sparingly, since food induces sleep.

5. Then the elders of the court delivered him to the elders of the priesthood. On taking their leave of him, they adjured him, saying, "My lord High Priest, we are delegates of the court and thou art our delegate and the delegate of the court.

We adjure thee by God that thou change naught of what we have said unto thee." The High Priest, thereupon, turned aside and wept, and they turned aside and wept.

6. If the High Priest was a scholar, he would expound scripture throughout the night. If not, the disciples of the sages would expound before him. They read out of the books of Job, Ezra, Chronicles and Daniel.

7. The young priests would divert him until the time of the sacrificing drew near to prevent fatigue and drowsiness.

8. In the morning, various offerings were made. The High Priest performed his various ministrations. In the morning, he wore raiment of gold and in the afternoon, he wore white garments. On this day he immersed himself in the ritual pool five times and he sanctified his hands and feet ten times.

9. After the High Priest made confession, he came to the east, to the north of the altar, with the Prefect on his right and the chief of his father's house on his left (the two highest ranking priests). There were the two he-goats and a casket containing two lots. He shook the casket and took up the lots. On one was written "For the Lord," and on the other, "For Azazel." He bound a thread of crimson wool on the head of the scapegoat and turned it toward the direction in which it was to be sent out. (Though thy sins be as scarlet, they shall be white as snow. Isaiah 1:18.) On the he-goat that was to be sacrificed, he bound a thread about its throat. He then made confession again over a bullock, his personal sin offering, and slaughtered it. He performed other ministrations, then went through the sanctuary until he reached the space between the two curtains separating the sanctuary from the Holy of Holies. He stepped inside the Holy of Holies, offered up a brief prayer, emerged quickly lest the people be worried, took the basin of blood (from the bullock) re-entered the Holy of Holies, sprinkled the blood once upwards and seven times downward while counting thus: one, one and one, one and two, one and three, one and four, one and five, one and six, one and seven.

On emerging, he put the basin of blood on the golden stand in the sanctuary. He then slaughtered the he-goat chosen by lot for the sacrifice, received its blood into a basin, re-entered the Holy of Holies, and again sprinkled and counted. Then followed a series of sprinklings outside and opposite the ark, on the golden altar, the outer altar and the inner altar and the cleansed surface of the altar, seven times.

10. When it was announced to the High Priest that the scapegoat had reached the wilderness, he proceeded to the *Ezras Noshim* (court of the women) and there read before the assembled people from a scroll of the law. He then pronounced eight benedictions: for the law, for the Temple service, for the thanksgiving, for the forgiveness of sin, for the Temple, for the Israelites, for the priests, and a general prayer for the rest. Afterwards he immersed himself in the ritual pool, sanctified his hands and feet, changed his garments, and was accompanied to his house by a throng. There a feast was held to celebrate his safe return from the sanctuary.

The *Avodah* service in the *Musaf* was intended to remind us of the glory of the Temple, the elaborate and dramatic sacrificial service of the priests attired in magnificent vestments, the mystifying ritual, the colorful processions, the poetic pageantry and choral singing of the Levites, the soul-stirring responses of the people in the courts of the Temple following breathlessly each gesture of the High Priest, especially the climax of the observances—the entry of the High Priest into the Holy of Holies. Although the sages wanted us to recall the grandeur of the Temple service, they did not seek a reenactment nor did they desire to retain any of the drama and ritual of the Temple. It is extremely difficult to reconstruct the motivation behind the profound change in Jewish worship wrought by the sages but it seems reasonable to assume that it was deliberate and influenced by the point of view of the prophets who clamored for greater emphasis on the spirit and less on the form, for greater sanctification of the commonplace and less lavish trappings, for more attention to the honest fervor and genuine zeal of the heart and mind of man in direct encounter with God and less stress on the supernatural. The sages felt the need for a creative revision which devalued the position of the priest, altar, censors, frying pans, incense, purifications, sprinklings, veils and other lavish, ornamental ac coutrements of the Temple and heightened the importance of active participation of the laity, of quiet and contemplative prayer, of Torah study within the service, of the quality of earnest simplicity.

The opening prayer of the *Avodah* in our service is the *Amitz Koach*, a *piyut* written by Rabbi Meshullam ben Kolonymus in Italy in the 10th century. It is an alphabetic acrostic combined with an acrostic in which the author spells out his name in the first letters of the final verses.

In the first part of the poem which runs from *aleph* to *pay* is described the order of creation, the dawn of history, the sinfulness of the early generations, the flood in the days of Noah, the patriarchs who make God known in the world, the birth of the Hebrew nation, the appointment of the Levites to minister in the Temple and of the High Priest to serve in the Holy of Holies, the seven day period of preparation during which he studies the books of Job, Ezra, Chronicles and Daniel, and the Day of Atonement observances.

The *Amitz Koach* does not explain why these four books were selected for the indoctrination of the High Priest but certainly the lessons of these books are related to the theme of Yom Kippur. The Book of Job, the classical story of an inno cent man's suffering, teaches us the importance of accepting adversity without losing faith in God. The Book of Ezra, the story of a man who inspired the Jewish people to rebuild from ruins amid desolate waste a thriving land and a Temple, teaches us how important it is to translate faith into acts of construction. The Book of Chronicles, reviews the story of mankind from Adam to the closing words of Cyrus, King of Persia, authorizing the rebuilding of the Temple in Jerusalem. It reminds us that man must acquire a realistic sense of history and reflect on his past ignominies as well as on past glories for the sake of his spiritual well-being. The Book of Daniel is the story of a man whose faith is tested in the fiery crucible of experience and emerges steadfast in the conviction that the future holds forth the great promise of redemption for all mankind.

The *pay* verse concludes with the High Priest setting his hands upon the bullock (his own sin offering) and making his confessions. At this point in the *Amitz Koach* is a break wherein is interpolated the *"v'Kach hoyoh omer,* this is what he said: O Lord, I have transgressed and sinned against Thee, I and my household. O Lord, forgive the sins, iniquities and transgressions which I and my household have committed in Thy sight, as it is written in the Torah of Thy servant Moses: 'On this day shall atonement be made for you, to purify you from all your sins before the Lord.' " This is immediately followed by the *v'hakohanim v'ho-om,* "When the priests and the people, who were standing in the Temple court, heard God's glorious and revered name clearly expressed by the high priest with holiness and purity, they fell on their knees, prostrated themselves and worshipped; they fell upon their faces and responded: 'Blessed be the name of His glorious majesty forever and ever.' "

The *Amitz* resumes with the *tsadik* verse in which we read of the drawing of lots by the high priest to select the scapegoat. The need for a scapegoat is deeply rooted in the nature of man. If misunderstood and unfulfilled, it can cause moral and spiritual disaster. Too much guilt feeling can shackle a man so he becomes incapable of exercising his free will. In his frantic effort to escape, he will palm off responsibility on someone or something other than himself and then seek to destroy the symbol of his guilt. Transferring his guilt does not help man escape its oppressive burden on his conscience. What man really wants and needs is vivid, convincing assurance of forgiveness. Once he removes the obsession of sin and guilt from his highly moral, sensitive conscience, he can concentrate on the steps leading to atonement and moral rehabilitation. The scapegoat ritual of the Day of Atonement provided a dramatic collective assurance that the burden of sin could be cast away. This was neither vicarious atonement nor transfer of guilt. It was simply acting out the powerful urge to banish excessive guilt that blocks the psyche from making right decisions and was only one step in the atonement process. After the high priest sends away the scapegoat, he returns to his own bullock a second time. This time he confesses not only his own sins but also those of his fellow priests. The interpolations following this verse parallel those following the preceding verse. "*V'kach hoyoh omer*—And this is what he said: 'O Lord, I and my household and the sons of Aaron have sinned . . . purify from . . .sins before the Lord.' " "*V'hakohanim v'ho-om*— When the priests and the people . . . 'Blessed be the name of all His glorious majesty forever and ever.' "

The *kuf* verses relate that as the high priest is about to enter the Holy of Holies, he is asked by the eldest priest whether he has searched his heart and repented, truly preparing himself to come before the Supreme King. The high priest replies that he has repented and urged his fellow priests to do likewise.

In the *resh* verses we read that the high priest, after slaughtering his bullock, enters the most holy place with an offering of incense and sprinkles the blood of his sin offering once upward and seven times downward. He then comes forth, slaughters the goat, re-enters the Holy of Holies and sprinkles its blood similarly.

In the *shin* verses we read that the high priest mingles the remaining blood of the two offerings, pours it upon the golden altar then hastens to the scapegoat. This time he makes confession for himself and the priests and the whole house of Israel. Interpolations like the two previous ones above, follow: *V'kach hoyoh omer*, "And this is what he said," and *v'hako-*

hanim v'ho-om, "When the priests and the people." The *shin verse* then continues the narrative of the high priest sending the scapegoat to the desert bearing the sins of Israel. The scapegoat is driven over the edge of a mountain. The use of a goat symbolized the idea that no individual is free from sin but by identifying individual sin with communal sin the individual can be released from the tormenting overpersonalization of guilt which drives men to complete and neurotic denial of guilt and responsibility. It was much easier for the ancient Jew to live with himself when he accepted the fact that everybody in t'e community, from the high priest down, sinned to some extent, but saw the effective ritual device which carried off communal sin so each man could start afresh and uncrushed by excessive accumulation of guilt feeling. This enabled him to assume responsibility fully and honestly for his behavior so he was under no inner compulsion to blame others in order to exonerate himself. The practice of finding and blaming a human scapegoat is morally repugnant and barbaric yet the tendency persists, even among civilized people. Ancient Israel's use of a goat had a humanizing, stabilizing effect which made responsibility for his behaviour the concern of each man.

In the concluding *shin* and *tuf* verses we read about the other sacrifices performed by the high priest, about the concluding ceremonies and about the joyful procession to the home of the high priest where the people celebrated the successful completion of his mission. In the name acrostic itself we read that the people, now purified and renewed, feels itself worthy to sing unto God.

The next prayer of the *Avodah* service, following the *Amitz Koach,* is the *Yehi Rotzon,* May it be Thy will. The high priest offers this prayer upon his safe completion of the Day of Atonement mission. It is an acrostic beginning with *aleph* and ending with *tuv.*

This is followed by the "*Mare Kohen,* The Countenance of the Priest," another alphabetic acrostic. This joyous poem describing the appearance of the priest as he emerges from the Holy of Holies, is based on the Book of Ecclesiasticus, Chapter 50. It describes the appearance of the High Priest Simon as he comes forth from the sanctuary: "Like the morning star shining in the east was the beaming countenance of the priest." The outlook and morale of leaders profoundly affect the spirit of the people particularly in times of uncertainty and fear.

"Ashre Ayin, Happy the eye that saw all this," is a poem based on a hymn by Solomon Ibn Gabirol, an 11th century poet and philosopher. It concludes with the lament that our soul is grieved because we are no longer privileged to witness the *Avodah* service of the Temple and to enjoy the general gladness attendant on the priest's bringing good tidings from the Holy of Holies.

The *Avodah* concludes with additional lamentations over the loss of the Temple, with prayers for the return of God's light and love to Zion, and a closing plea for forgiveness.

THE MARTYROLOGY

(A-178 to 183; B-837 to 847; S-381 to 391)

The martyrology is still another part of the middle section of the *Amidah.* It is the story of the ten sages who suffered martyrdom and is, in essence, the story of the Jewish people's dignity and nobility maintained at a cost of pain and death throughout the ages. The torture was borne bravely for a noble cause.

Our whole religious literature is the story of a people's attempt, in the intellectual and spiritual areas of life, to explain and to alleviate human suffering. The compulsive force behind the discovery of prayer, the search for God, the centrality of knowledge, the tears of the prophets denouncing injustice, the efforts of the rabbis promulgating laws of charity and righteousness was, and is, the passion to prevent and to mitigate suffering.

What has made the Jew so sensitive to human distress? Who has designated him the suffering servant of God? Many nations have suffered but inflicted suffering on others at the first opportunity. As a result of his own suffering, the Jew has developed an acute awareness of the suffering of others. The Jewish people escaped the psychological and dehumanizing effects of suffering by interpreting their suffering as necessary for the defense of an ideal which made life itself worthwhile. His suffering had purpose. Martyrdom, heroic self-sacrifice for a noble cause, always calls forth admiration and reverence rather than the normal reaction of sympathy and pity at the sight of death, the negation of life.

The word "martyr" is the Greek word for "witness." The martyr is one who feels that his whole life must bear witness to the supreme value of his ideal and that his conduct would be a *Hillul Hashem,* a profanation of God's name, if he surrendered his principles under pressure. The martyr, proof against intimidation, makes his death a triumphant affirmation of the values of life. Unlike Christianity which worships one who martyred himself for God's children, Judaism worships a God for whom His children martyred themselves.

The *"Eleh Ezkera*—these martyrs I will remember," of the martyrology is an alphabetic acrostic poem of four line stanzas. The author has never been definitely identified although the same acrostic and the same signature at the conclusion of the poem is appended to other *piyutim.* The poem is based on an event which took place in Palestine during the Roman occupation. Ten great sages of Israel defied the imperial edict of the Roman Emperor Hadrian, which forbade the founding of schools and the teaching of Torah, and were tortured to death. Submission to Roman intimidation would have meant abandonment of the high principal of Judaism that life is not worthwhile without the study of God's word.

Akiba, one of the ten martyrs, died at the stake with the statement: "It is written, 'And thou shalt love the Lord thy God with all thy life.' Now I know how to interpret this verse which puzzled me heretofore. It means, *even if thy life be de-*

manded." Another, Hananiah ben Teradion, was burned at the stake wrapped in the *Sefer Torah* out of which he had given instruction. His last words were: "I see the parchment burning but the letters of the Torah are flying heavenward." He died to reaffirm the indestructability of God's commandments.

Modern scholars have had considerable difficulty with this prayer because it makes no reference to the Hadrianic ban on Torah study as the reason for the execution of these martyrs. It states that the Emperor, after reading the story of Joseph and his brothers, asked the sages what punishment is meted out to those guilty of kidnapping. The sages replied that the death is the penalty for stealing another human. Whereupon, the Emperor ordered the ten sages to expiate the sin of the ten brothers of Joseph. The difficulty with this dirge is twofold.

First, why was the historical reference to the Hadrianic ban on Torah omitted and the death of the sages attributed to a cause involving Jewish culpability? This tendency to explain our misfortunes in terms of our own shortcomings, rather than by shifting the blame elsewhere, is more in keeping with our character and the spirit of self-judgment. We have always asked ourselves, what did we do or fail to do that might have prevented the calamity? For example, the sages blamed the destruction of the Temple on the disunity in our own ranks, not on the Romans. The rabbis taught us not to blame the Babylonians or the Romans for our exile from the land but *mipne chatoeynu,* because of our own sins. Were they unaware of the external forces bearing upon our adversity? No. In their wisdom they realized that self-judgment could lead to self-improvement, positive action in the right direction, whereas placing the blame on others, no matter how culpable they may actually be, is a negative satisfaction of the ego. In this manner, every misfortune was transformed into a blessing.

The second difficulty arises from the fact that the moral philosophy of the dirge is inconsistent with the generally accepted Jewish view that descendants should not expiate the sins of their ancestors. However, if we interpret the poem partly as a protest against those who persist in persecuting the innocent for the real or imaginary sins of their ancestors, this difficulty also drops away.

THE CONFESSION
(A-184 to 188; B-849 to 857; S-393 to 397)

The final section of the middle blessing of the *Amidah* is the confession which is made up of two alphabetical acrostics, the *Oshamnu* and the *Al Chet*. The value of confession was clear to the rabbis. However, they were not in favor of confessing sins to a fellow human being. Rather they taught that man should confess his sins only to God. Today it has become fashionable to tell the psychiatrist everything and to keep secrets from God. This is very unfortunate because our peace of soul depends, not on the psychiatrist, but on divine forgiveness. Much of contemporary emotional disturbance arises from our failure to talk with God. The confession part of the Musaf is designed to encourage the Jew to reveal his sins to God.

"Ashamnu—we are guilty," is a very old prayer. It is brief and decisive, using few words to express the manifold ways in which man sins against God. By studying them very carefully we can become keenly aware of the moods, attitudes and acts that estrange us from God.

The pre-modern man knew that he sinned and, therefore, had to seek forgiveness from God. Reconciliation with God is far more difficult for modern man. He has been taught that he is not to blame for his faults, that his mistakes are due to faulty upbringing, inadequate parents, unsound teachers, an insane society, an unfortunate environment, adverse accidents, insufficient love in infancy, too much parental concern, and a host of other external factors. Modern man has thus been absolved of guilt and relieved of responsibility. This type of absolution, carried to its current extreme, has done much to damage man's soul. The lack of guilt feeling and the denial of responsibility often leads to psychological confusion and moral delinquency. In a very real sense many people feel guilty because they have no conscious feelings of guilt. Normal and conscious guilt feelings, suppressed or interpreted out of existence, threaten to become dangerous,neurotic guilt. The normal man of normal impulse must have a normal recognition of right and wrong which leads to awareness of sin. Man's moral improvement depends on his recognition of sin and guilt and of the need for confession and correction.

Too much guilt feeling can be as devastating as too little. Excessive dwelling on sin and guilt leads to pathological self-reduction. People who debase themselves are rendered unworthy and incapable of glorifying God. People who consider themselves worthless sinners cannot be morally effective. People who have no faith in themselves cannot rise spiritually. Our religion teaches us that in regard to sin and guilt we must avoid both unconsciousness and obsession. We should feel guilty but we must free ourselves of excessive guilt. This is beautifully illustrated in the Hasidic explanation for the alphabetic listing of the sins in the *Ashamnu* and in the *Al Chet*. "If it were otherwise, we would not know when to stop beating our breasts, for there is no end to sin and no end to being aware of sin, but there is an end to the alphabet."

"Al Chet—For the sins which we have committed before Thee," is a longer confessional. Note the plural subject throughout. When people learn to confess their own sins and to overlook the mistakes of others, instead of the other way round, perhaps the world will be ready for the coming of the Messiah. In this sense, there is a messianic suggestion in the *Al Chet*. The refrain at the conclusion of each section of the *Al Chet*, "For all these, O God of forgiveness, *forgive* us, *pardon* us, *grant* us *atonement*," suggests the three stages of complete rehabilitation from sin through *Tfillah* (prayer), *T'Shuvah* (repentance) and *Tzedakah* (charity). Translated into modern psychological terminology, the first stage would involve self-

155

evaluation, the second, reeducation to new perspectives, and the third, new motivation to independence and assurance against relapse.

THE THREE FINAL BENEDICTIONS OF THE AMIDAH
(A-191 to 196; B-863 to 877; S-400 to 403)

These three brief benedictions of thanksgiving follow in rapid succession and conclude the *Amidah* of the Great Day just as they do on Sabbaths and weekdays. In ancient times, the first one, which begins with the word *Retsay,* was a prayer of thanskgiving for the Temple service. Since the destruction of the Temple, it has been a prayer of petition for the restoration of the *Shechinah* (God's presence) to Zion. The second blessing begins with the words, *Modim anachnu loch,* we gratefully acknowledge Thee. The final and greatest blessing is the blessing in which we thank God for peace. The last word of the entire *Amidah* is *sholom,* peace, in order that we may remember it, use it wisely, perpetuate it with all our resources.

12

Yom Kippur Mincha Service

The *Minchah* service is always a very brief one. On Yom Kippur it consists of the following:

1. Opening of the Holy Ark (*Psichat HaAron*)
2. Reading of the Torah (*Kriat HaTorah*)
3. The *Amidah*
4. *Kaddish*.

THE TORAH READING (*Leviticus* 18)

(A-199; B-885; S-409)

The three main points of the Torah portion, which deals with marriage and sexual purity, are:

1) Marriages which are permissible are distinguished from those which are forbidden.

2) Sexual perversion, e.g., sodomy, homosexuality, etc., and adultery are banned.

3) Sexual relations with one's own wife are prohibited during the menstrual cycle, on fast days and during a period of mourning.

Forbidden marriages and the other forbidden practices indicated above were considered abomination. Such abominations were considered the cause of the downfall of nations. "For all these abominations have the men of the land done which were before you . . . that the land vomit you not out also as it vomited out the nations that went before you."

157

Family purity is the very core of Judaism. Some of the chief tenets of our faith have been concerned with the purity and moral integrity of Jewish family life. The keyword of Jewish marriage is *Kiddushin,* sanctification and separation from things impure. In our tradition the home is referred to as the small sanctuary. The sacred nature of wedlock demands self-control and right conduct in intimate marital relations. Sexual discipline and wholesome family relations were stressed from earliest biblical days.

The biblical laws governing marriage and sex invested Jewish life with strengths and values, such as:

1) Fostering sexual discipline

2) Protecting physical and mental health

3) Clear attitudes, firm values, strong principles and definite standards in a vital area of living

4) Divorce and infidelity were negligible

5) Family unity and compatibility were rooted firmly on moral and spiritual grounds

It is abundantly and all-too-painfully clear that divorce, infidelity and confusion are making devastating inroads on Jewish family life. Strong family feeling still distinguishes the Jewish people but the Jewish family has felt the effects of the general corrosion and breakdown of family life throughout our society. Like our predecessors, we need in Jewish life today a conception of *Taharat Hamishpachah,* purity of the family. We must recognize the fatal error of rejecting the cornerstone which is the foundation of family stability and happiness.

This passage from the Bible is read on Yom Kippur to remind us that impurity, promiscuity, perversion, unchastity and unbridled passion are serious offenses calling down punishment from Heaven of the individual offender and of the society that permits such offenses.

Haftorah Reading—Book of Jonah
(A-201; B-889; S-411)

The storm raged and the ship was threatened because "Jonah had fled from the presence of the Lord." The lesson of this section from the Book of Jonah is self-evident: When we fail in our duties toward one another by evading social responsibilities, we invite disaster. Storms of hatred and violence, war and destruction, have threatened to overwhelm us in the past due to our failure to accept our responsibilities. Such storms will threaten and break until we all come to recognize that those different from us racially, culturally, and socially are also God's children deserving love and care and sacrifice on our part. When Jonah was sent by God to speak to the people of Nineveh, he refused because they were ignorant, pagan and strangers. Why should he put himself out to help them? Thus he sought to flee.

The Book of Jonah offers hope for our times. Not only was the prophet Jonah forgiven but also the wicked city of Nineveh when its peoples prayed to God and returned to Him in sincere penitence. If we learn well the messages of the Torah and Haftorah readings and apply them honestly and intelligently, we will come to grips with the social forces that divide our families and weaken the unity of mankind today.

Repetition of the Amidah
(A-215 to 42; B-915 to 53; S-425 to 41)

In the middle of the first blessing, "Blessed art Thou . . . Shield of Abraham," is inserted a prayer forming an acrostic from *Aleph* (one) to *Yud* (ten) (initial letters of each verse when read down, form the first ten letters of the Hebrew alphabet). The conclusion of the prayer is a plea by the congregation that God pardon us for the sake of the righteousness of the virtuous patriarch Abraham. The reference by the cantor to the grove planted by Abraham where he proclaimed God's mighty deeds is based on a Midrash. After hungry wayfarers partook of the fruits of the trees and thanked Abraham therefore, he would reply, "Do not thank me. Thank God who feeds and sustains us all."

In the second blessing, "Blessed art Thou . . . Givest life to the dead," is inserted another 10-verse acrostic by Elijah ben Mordechai, from *mem* through *tuv*. (This and the previous prayer were probably one acrostic of the full alphabet originally.) The reference here is to the virtue of Isaac who permitted his father Abraham to bind him on the altar as a sacrifice to God. The hand of Abraham was stayed by God who does not desire this type of sacrifice. Man should indeed be willing to die for the supreme values of life but God wishes his children to live for him. The cantor asks God to spare us because of father Isaac's righteousness so that we may be able to serve Him.

The third blessing, "Blessed art Thou . . . the Holy King," is introduced with a *piyut* in which the first letter of each phrase, taken in order, spell out the name of the author, Elijah ben Mordechai. The reference here is to the virtue of the third patriarch, Jacob. According to the Midrash, Jacob's image was engraved on God's throne. When Jacob (also called Israel) on his deathbed summoned his children, he had the feeling that they were divided among themselves. They assured him that they were united in belief by exclaiming with one voice: "Hear, O Israel, the Lord our God, the Lord is One." On this day, likewise, we assure our Father in heaven that we cast away the petty differences and rending hates that sunder men from one another and from God. The cantor asks God to spare us because of Jacob's virtue.

The alphabetic acrostic which follows is an introduction to the *kedushah* which is based on Isaiah's vision of the angels in heaven worshipping God. The *piyut* introducing the *kedushah* amplifies it. Like the angels in heaven we also rise to glorify God with the three-fold sanctification: "Holy, Holy, Holy is the Lord of Hosts." Redemption is hereby dramatized. What is redemption? It is man's eternal seeking to realize his highest spiritual potential as "but little lower than the angels."

The fourth (middle) blessing of this seven-blessing *Amidah* is long and elaborate. It begins with the *Ato V'Chartanu,* "Thou has chosen us," and concludes with "Blessed art Thou . . . Who sanctifies Israel and the Day of Atonement." The following ideas or themes are enunciated in the succession of one-paragraph prayers that constitute this section of the fourth *Bracha:*

1. God bestowed upon Israel the responsibility of keeping His commandments, the privilege to worship Him and the honor of being called by His name as a concomitant to His choosing Israel.

2. The Day of Atonement is an opportunity to obtain forgiveness, a gift of God's love.

3. The day of deliverance for Zion will be a great day of reconciliation with God.

4. The covenant between God and Israel implies that forgiveness is always forthcoming.

5. The *"Shema Kolenu," "Ki Anu Amecho V'Ato Elohenu,"* and *"Al Chet"* all appear in this fourth blessing because they relate to the theme of blessing, "Blessed art Thou . . . Who maketh holy the Day of Atonement." These have all been commented on sufficiently elsewhere.

The last three blessings are the familiar conclusion of every *Amidah:*

"Blessed art Thou . . . Who restores His presence unto Zion."

"Blessed art Thou . . . unto Thee it is good to give praise."

"Blessed art Thou, O Lord, Who makes peace."

The Ark is closed, the congregation seated, and the *Kaddish* concludes the service.

13

The Neilah Service

In the Jewish prayer book there are three services daily—morning, afternoon and evening; four on the Sabbath and on holidays. This extra service is known as the *Musaf* or additional service. The only day in the year when we have five services is the Day of Atonement. This fifth service is called *Neilah* meaning, literally, "closing."

The final service was called Neilah because it was recited at the hour when the gates of the Temple in Jerusalem were about to be closed thus marking the end of a long day of worship. According to another explanation, it is so called because the service is recited at the hour when the Gates of Heaven are about to be shut and the people, exhausted by fasting and prayer, make a final supreme effort to reach the heart of God, to penetrate the gates of mercy, and to obtain the favor of Providence.

At *Neilah* the prayer in which we have been asking to be *inscribed* in the Book of Life is modified to read *sealed* in the Book of Life. We have finished pleading our case by the end of the day and the decision of the fate of each individual is now ready to be fixed and sealed.

The ark remains open and the congregation stands during the entire service. Special melodies and chants which breathe of hope and confidence characterize the service and the conclusion is marked by jubilation and optimism. After the final *Kaddish* is recited, the reader and the congregation chant in unison and in exultation the *"Shema."* The phrase "Blessed be the Name of His Kingdom forever and ever" is chanted three times and, finally, "the Lord is King" is proclaimed loudly seven times whereupon the loud, long blast of the *shofar* declares that the day has come to a close. Thus, the concluding service of the day ends on an impressive, highly dramatic note.

THE NEILAH AMIDAH

Aimé Pallière, a French Catholic studying for the priesthood, describes his reaction to the first Jewish service he attended. He had entered the synagogue at the time of the *Neilah Amidah.*

"That which revealed itself to me at that moment was not the Jewish faith. It was the Jewish people. The spectacle of that large number of Jewish men assembled, their shoulders covered by the *Talith* (prayer shawl), suddenly disclosed to my eyes a far-off past. The Hebrews of the Bible were there on their feet before me. Two details struck me particularly about the faithful bent over their ritual. At first, on seeing the prayer shawls worn uniformly by all the participants in the service, I thought that in a way they were all officiating. In the second place, it seemed to me that this silent assembly was in expectancy of something to happen. 'What are they waiting for?' I asked my companion. Here were revealed to me two characteristics of this misunderstood people and its great faith: the form of collective priesthood which characterizes Judaism, and the spirit of expectancy and of faith in the future which stamps its entire cult with a special zeal."

"In the Synagogue service, all Jews are equal, all are priests, all may participate, all may officiate. Had my attention not been captured by this spectacle of a multitude of men wrapped with shawls and enrapt in prayer, this peculiarity of Judaism would have escaped me. It is thus that rites and symbols often constitute a more expressive language than the best of discourses. The practices of the Jewish religion which have had the consecration of centuries come to us charged with the accumulated thoughts of believing generations. They preserve the poetry, the incomparable power of evocation. They may be suppressed but not replaced."

"A precious legacy of antiquity, and yet, Judaism's trend is not toward the past but toward the future. An unconquerable faith in the final triumph of the good and the true has preserved it during the centuries and permeates it. It awaits the Messiah . . . Whenever and wherever the modern conscience busies itself with the ideals of social regeneration, whenever it affirms its will to build the city of the future upon the ruins of wrongs and injustices, it is in communion with the soul of Judaism. Later I was to understand what this spirit of expectancy was and what the people waited for in the closing moments of the silent prayer of the Neilah service. Yet, here was the beginning of my realization that the Christian concept of the Jew was wrong, that Israel still has a right to live, that Israel still has a mission, that Israel still lives."

THE OPENING PRAYER

(A-243; B-957; S-448)

The first prayer of the Neilah service is Psalm 145, *Ashre,* which opens the *Mincha* Service on weekdays. This Psalm of Praise of David in which is an affirmation that the source of happiness is God, is a fitting opening to this concluding service of the Day of Atonement. It is in the form of an alphabetic acrostic from which only the letter *nun,* the first letter of *"nafal"* (fallen), is omitted. From the standpoint of Judaism and the spirit of the services on this Holy Day, man should not be called "fallen." Man may temporarily fall away from the highest moral and spiritual standards and become demoralized in his thinking and behavior but he can rise again through repentance and atonement to achieve the blessings that God has prepared for all those who call upon Him in truth. God is the source of happiness but the individual is responsible for attaining it. The *Ashre* is taken verbatim from the Book of Psalms and is followed by the Half-Kaddish.

THE NEILAH AMIDAH

(A-246 to 252; B-963 to 975; S-451 to 457)

The first three benedictions are the same as those appearing in all other *Amidos*. The middle, or fourth, blessing is "Blessed art Thou . . . who sanctifies Israel and the Day of Atonement." Then follows the confessional *"Ashamnu."* The *"Al Chet"* is replaced by two special prayers more in keeping with the mood of *Neilah*: the *"Atah Noten*—Thou givest a hand to transgressors and Thy right hand is stretched out to receive the penitent;" and the *"Atah Hivdaltah*—Thou hast distinguished man from the beginning and hast recognized his privilege that he might stand before Thee."

ATAH NOTEN

This picture of the merciful Father reaching out His hand to His repentant children is in harmony with the Jewish conception of God. However, the description of man as a worm, and human striving as vanity is not the predominant Jewish view of the meaning of life. This note of philosophic despair rarely appears in the Sacred Writings or in the liturgy; it crops up in *Koheleth* and just a few Psalms. Our religion does assert that God is absolute and omnipotent but does not disparage man. The tendency to depreciate man in order to glorify God is understandable but should not be taken seriously as a philosophy of life. Truly God is our Master and we are His servants. But we are servants possessing personality and worth. We fulfill our duty to obey but serve Him best when we are aware that our efforts count for something, when we serve with dignity.

ATAH HIVDALTAH

This prayer is much closer to the predominant moral mood of Judaism than the *"Atah Noten."* Man's distinction arises from his ability to discern right from wrong, and to repent and change his course of action when he errs. The prayer consists of a number of Biblical verses expressing the view that man has the power to release himself from sin, and a merciful God stands ever ready to help him.

REPETITION OF THE AMIDAH
(A-253 to 268; B-977 to 1011; S-459 to 475)

At the conclusion of the silent *Amidah,* the Ark is opened and the repetition of the *Amidah* is begun. The cantor chants the *"Mesod"* announcing his intention to implore God's forgiveness.

The first plea for forgiveness is based on the virtues of our fathers Abraham, Isaac and Jacob. *"Av Yeda-ucha"*—Though God tested Abraham with ten crises, each one of which would have shattered the faith of a lesser man, Abraham continued to seek God. Maltreated by his contemporaries, Abraham yet urged the stranger and wayfarer to partake of his hospitality. He stood at the door of his tent even in the heat of the day to welcome them. Like Abraham, who never lost faith in God the Father and man the brother, we ever seek to enter the presence of God and to find our brothers.

The second, *"Hanikra L'Av*—He in whom his father's seed was called,"* refers to Isaac who met Rebecca as he "went out to meditate in the field at eventide." Fulfillment came to Isaac who first spoke prayer in the evening; so may God grant favorable answers to his seed.

"Teva Ziv—The form of Jacob's beauteous countenance"* is a reference to Jacob who dreamed of a wondrous ladder extending from heaven to earth, of a God who descends to earth for man's guidance and protection, of men who can ascend to God through faith and virtue.

These three brief responsive prayers allude to the *"Zehus Avos,"* the merit of the fathers, on the strength of which we ask God to forgive us. This concept of children benefitting by the merit of the fathers is in sharp contrast to the doctrine of original sin which stamps each soul at birth with sin because it is descended from father Adam who was guilty of the original sin.

The second appeal to God is for our own virtues and aspirations. *"Shaare Armon*—Open the Gates of the Temple and of Heaven and let us sanctify Thee with the mystic words of the angels who hallow Thy name with the words of the *'Kedushah,'* the prayer of Holiness,"* is reminiscent of the Prophet Isaiah's picture of the angels standing before the Throne of Glory chanting these mystic words to God. Similarly, the entire congregation stands, the men wrapped in prayer shawls, chanting with fervor each syllable of the *Kedushah* in a final, stirring effort to break through the Gates to God. *"Psach Lanu Shaar*—Open the Gates for us. Yea, even at the closing of the gates. For day is nearly past, the day is passing thus. The sun is low, the day is growing late. O let us into Thy gate at last."

The appeal that follows is for forgiveness because of God's virtues, His thirteen attributes of mercy. The prayers and *piyutim* express the theme that hope for forgiveness and reconciliation depend, in the final analysis, on God's mercy. Our fathers and the spiritual traditions they bequeathed to us, our own significant efforts and virtues, are all part of the drama of redemption which process is not complete without God.

THE 13 ATTRIBUTES OF GOD'S MERCY

The thirteen attributes of God restated here in our *Mahzor* were given to us in the second book of the Torah, in Exodus 34:6-7.

1) God is merciful to one who has the intention and is about to sin. Even as the sinful act is contemplated, God's mercy continues to function as a deterrent.

2) God is forgiving to the sinner who has repented.

3) God is powerful to act as His wisdom dictates. In His

wisdom he has granted man moral freedom to choose between right and wrong without losing any part of His all-powerfulness.

4) God is as kind as a father to his children. Without discouraging their initiative and freedom, he tries to prevent them from sinning.

5) God is gracious to those who have fallen, and assists them to rise.

6) God is patient and ever hopeful that the sinner will repent.

7) God is generous both to the righteous and the wicked.

8) God is truthful and faithful to carry out his promises.

9) God performs acts of lovingkindness to thousands and gives them credit for the merit of their fathers.

10) God forgives sins committed even with premeditation.

11) God forgives sins committed in the spirit of rebellion against Him.

12) God forgives sins committed inadvertantly.

13) God not only forgives but "wipes the slate clean."

"Eloheynu, Velohe Avoseynu—Our God and God of our Fathers," is an 11-stanza prayer composed by Solomon ben Judah, the Babylonian, in the 10th century. The theme is a reassertion that we cannot achieve victory over sin, and peace of conscience, without the help of God.

Rabbi Solomon, the son of Judah, was a prolific writer of *piyutim* and *selichot*. Many of them were incorporated in various *Machzorim*. Most of his poems are alphabetic acrostics both in straight order from *Aleph* to *Tuf*, and in reverse order from *Tuf* to *Aleph*. This particular *piyut* is non-acrostic.

Rabbi Solomon was called the Babylonian even though he never was in Babylon. He lived and wrote in Rome.

"Zchor Bris—Remember the Covenant," is part of a *Selicha*, penitential prayer, written by Gershon bar Judah at the beginning of the 11th century. The appeal here is "Save us for Thy name's sake."

During the 11th and 12th centuries, the number of *paitanim* reached several hundred. These great legal and intellectual masters, codifiers of the law and commentators of the Talmud, found a perfect vehicle for expressing their deepest emotions and sensitive religious feelings in poetry. When not engaged in the constructive work of the intellect (law), they expressed in *piyutim* and *selichot* the need for faith to sustain them during the holocaust of the Middle Ages. One of these great scholars, the *paitan* Gershom ben Jehudah (960-1028) known also as the "Light of the Exile," poured forth his soul in fiery speech. His own son was brutally murdered in one of the many massacres of the Medieval period. Like the other *paitanim,* Rabbenu Gershom complains in his poetry to God, protests against suffering, asks the reason for the affliction. At the same time, he brought hope and comfort to the heart of the oppressed.

Gershom ben Jehuda was born in France. Later he settled in Mayence, Germany, where he started an Academy, a college for the study of the Talmud. He was responsible for some of the most important decrees (*Takanot*) in Jewish religious and social matters. His most famous *Takanah* is the prohibition of polygamy among Ashkenazic Jews.

"*Enkas M'Salodecho*—The cry of those who praise Thee," consists of four brief verses, the beginnings of 4 different *piyutim* by four *paitanim,* built around the verse "*Adonoy, Adonoy,*" which enumerate the thirteen attributes of God's mercy and which serve as a refrain. In all probability, the complete *piyutim* were recited by the congregation when time permitted, only the first verses when time was short. The complete stanzas no longer exist, only the first verses have been preserved from the 11th-13th centuries when they were originally written.

"*Ezkira Elohim*—I remember, O God," is a four stanza poem written by Ammitai ben Shefatiah in the 11th century.

169

In the first stanza the destruction of Jerusalem is lamented; in the second is a plea for God's mercy to intercede in our behalf; in the third is confession of our reliance upon God's thirteen attributes and the merit of our fathers to save us; in the fourth is an appeal to God to hear our weeping and to deliver us from dreaded decrees.

In the final plea to "Open the Gates of Heaven," we repeat for the last time the confessional, the *Ashamnu,* and the *Avinu Malkenu.*

Then follows a dramatic conclusion, the three professions of Faith:

1) The *Shema Yisroel* which we say only once because there is only one God.

2) *"Boruch Shem*—Blessed be His Kingdom," which we repeat three times after the chazan because His Kingdom extends over the past, present and the future.

3) *"Adonoy Hu Elohim*—God is King," which we repeat seven times as a symbol of the seven Heavens God opened when he reached out and gave us the Torah, and which He opens to our prayers so we may reach to His very Throne to receive His forgiveness.

After we exclaim: "Next year in Jerusalem," the chazan starts a spirited chanting of the *Kaddish.* Immediately before the *"Tiskabel"* of the *Kaddish,* the *shofar* is sounded. One long, exultant *"Tekiah,"* suggests victory in our spiritual battle and expresses our happy confidence that God has forgiven and sealed us for a good New Year.

INDEX

INDEX

INDEX

Maftir, 68
Maimonides, Moses, 23, 72
Malachi, 11
Malchuyos, 87
Man, 127-128
  Brotherhood of, 106
  dependence on God, 105
  free moral agent, 48
  his distinction, 165
  his goal, 105
  nature of, 39, 60, 82, 83
  not fallen, 164
  source of his significance, 40
  tested not trapped, 106
Marriage, 157
Martyrology, 151
Meaning and Mystery, 26
Meir of Rothenburg, 104
Mercy, 13
  attributes of God's, 167-168
  seat of, 79
Meshulam ben Kalonymos, 80, 127, 129, 141
Messiah, 26, 164
Messianic Age, 48
Messianic Vision, 57
Midrash, 159
Mi Sheberach, 68
Mishnah, 144
Mitzvos, 33, 52
Monotheism, 106
Morality, 48

Natronai Gaon, 2
Nature, 50
  conception of, 60
Neilah, reason for name, 162

Obedience, 124
Olenu, 143
Omnipotence, 140
Original sin, 166

Paitanim, 4
Pallière, Aimé, 163
Parenthood, 107-108
Peace, 20, 63, 64, 84
Piyutim, 54, 77
  Rabbinic opposition to, 4-5
  types of, 126
Pope, 49
Praise of God, 44-45
Prayer, efficacy of, 54, 112
  for dead, 134-137
  importance of, 25

  moods of, 107
  position during, 143
  praise before petition, 44
  preparation for, 102
  position for, 102-103
  types of, 119
  unworthy, 111
Prayer Books, origin and development of, 2
Prayers, dates of, 4
Priesthood, collective, 163
Prophets, false and true, 116
Psalms of the day, 42-43
Psychiatry, 59
Psychology, of guilt, 154-155

Rabbi of Nemerov, 5
Rav, 85, 143
Redeemer, 139
Redemption, 63, 160-161, 167
  historical evidence of, 53
  through Mitvos, 53
Religion, 103, 124
Repentence, 96-97
Repetition, value of, 125
Responsibility, 89, 109, 116, 159
  basis of morality, 79
Restoration, 64
Revelation, 26, 62
Righteousness, ultimate victory of, 48
Ritual, changes, 131
  language of religion, 132
  values of, 132

Saadiah Gaon, 2
Sacrifice, 40-41, 69-71
Salvation, 94
Sanctification, 63-64
  of God's name, 141
Scapegoat, 146
  meaninb of, 148
Security, 33
Self, 22
Self-judgment, 59, 153
Selichos, 5, 126
Septuagint, 129
Sex, 157
Shalom, 156
Shield of Abraham, 15
Shofar, 102
  meaning of, 73-75
  final blast of, 163, 170
  period of blowing, 14-15
Shofros, 88-89
Simcha ben Samuel, 3
Simeon ben Isaac, 49, 57

173

INDEX